D0107978

GAYLE D. ERWIN

YAHSHUA
PUBLISHING

Not Many Mighty

YAHSHUA Publishing
PO Box 219
Cathedral City, CA 92235-0219
Phone 1-888-321-0077
FAX 760-202-1139

Printed in the United States of America.
Cover by Dempster Evans

Table of Contents

Part Three
A Heart for the Flawed

High and Mighty

An Introduction

Every man's culture influences his spiritual understanding. European intellectualism and skepticism blind them to the simple Gospel they once vigorously spread. Buddhists long ago abandoned the celibacy taught by their founder. Hinduism's lack of a system of beliefs forces them into whatever the latest guru or brahmin demands.

The United States, the remaining super power, often operates church from the position of power and competitiveness. Being a USA citizen, born the child of a pastor thus intimate observer of the church scene and observer around the world, I write of what I see best.

We Americans often abandon our discernment whenever persons of note, whether in sports, cinema or politics, declare themselves to be Christian. Such a person, who garners TV and press time, thrills us and validates our own lives. If nothing else, it proves, in our minds, that we, as the Church, are just as good as anybody else and maybe a bit better—just look at who has joined us.

We glory in massive buildings whose architecture, while wasteful, proclaims to the world that we are as rich and as influential as anyone. Church and religious magazines feature the best looking, the achiever, the winner, sometimes people whose only achievement is a beautiful body or a natural athletic capability.

At what point do we hear and believe Paul's statements in 1 and 2 Corinthians: *"Not many mighty, not many noble"* or *"God has chosen the weak things to confuse the mighty and the foolish things to confuse the wise"*? At what point do we notice that the *"common people, the poor people of the land"* heard Jesus gladly? (Mark 12:37 KJV)

In countless conferences and retreats, I have publicly taken notice that the governor was not present. Nor was the lieutenant governor. Not even a mayor. No press cameras roamed around. Then, in driving the humorous point home, I would ask, "Who are you people? They promised me a quality crowd." Usually, no one had even bothered to take notice since such persons of prominence were rarely around in the spiritual scene (unless, of course, an election campaign was going on).

The simple fact is that the common people still hear him gladly even though our culture elevates the rich, the famous, the powerful even in the church. I have long held that the church is supported by poor people. I tell pastors that if they have a rich person in their church, he will become the greatest headache. When have you seen a rich person in the church simply give anonymously? No, they often use their funds to manipulate and threaten. I continue to marvel at the fact that the poorest state in the United States holds the position of giving the most to *charity* as described by the government.

Perhaps it is best that we continue to not notice the true gathering of God's people and continue to withhold honor from the genuine kingdom populace. Maybe therein lies a secret of preventing corruption.

This brings me to the reason for this book. The influence of cultural heroism along with our high regard for the Bible and its characters greatly impacts our beliefs and, consequently, our decision-making. We tend to place our biblical heroes on a pedestal—a position of communication with God and closeness to him that we feel is beyond our reach.

James, perhaps in an effort to do for readers what I am trying to do, informs us in 5:17 that Elijah was a man with a nature just like us. That declaration by James becomes the effort of this book. Basically, I want to show that the heroes of the Bible were as incompetent as I am. Their claim to fame, while real, was simply the grace of God showing whom he chooses to use and how his availability and power continue to flow to the *little* man.

PART ONE

Flawed Patriarchs Flawed Prophets

Brothers, think of what you were when you were called.
Not many of you were wise by human standards; not many were influential; not many were of noble birth.
But God chose the foolish things of the world to shame the wise;
God chose the weak things of the world to shame the strong.
He chose the lowly things of this world and the despised things–and the things that are not–to nullify the things that are, so that no one may boast before him.
1 Corinthians 1:26–29

What is highly valued among men is detestable in God's sight.
Luke 16:15

Chapter 1

Adam's Perfect Chance

Few people view Adam as a hero, but his record was as good as anyone else's. He was the original, the "image of God" man. His home? A perfect gated community! His opportunities? Limitless! His achievement? Walking with God. His challenge? A phenomenal tree called the *Tree of Life* whose fruit granted eternal life! His courtship? Not a moment of struggle! His wife? Especially made for him by God! Their wardrobe? Empty but adequate! Food? Varied and limitless! Surely there were billions of trees in that perfect garden—all of them edible. Life could not be better.

Capping off that perfect life, God asked only that Adam and Eve tend the garden and follow one rule, only one. Avoid one tree in the middle of the garden—the Tree of the Knowledge of Good and Evil, because if you eat of it you will die. So, out of billions of trees, all edible, only one was to be avoided. What a simple rule. No ten commandments, no list of curses, no complex set of laws. Only one rule: Don't eat from that tree!

Two problems clouded that issue. First, God created man with the power of choice. That power must have been the "image of God" in creation. I doubt that God was short, plump and bald as I am. But our highest capability is that of choice. So, to exercise that image, God presented the choice.

Second, the Tree of the Knowledge of Good and Evil was probably the most beautiful one in the garden—at least it's fruit looked the best. Perhaps it was chocolate covered. At any rate, the next thing we see, Adam and Eve sitting under that tree, observing and wondering. Perhaps they were asking themselves why God would keep them from the best looking tree. Perhaps they were thinking that God didn't love them to treat them this way. Perhaps the prospect of the knowledge of evil titillated them as much as it does humans today.

Whenever we ask, "Why would God...?" Satan loves to join the conversation. He is a theologian, you know. His appearances in Scripture are proof. I think he must have been a seminary graduate. I think I know which seminary. Well, you know the rest. Their best logic failed them. They ate and changed swiftly from their joyous former status.

Shame Plus

Now they knew shame. Now they hid from God. Now they were ejected from the garden. Now no access to the Tree of Life. Now the ground that had been their friend became their enemy. Now Adam had to dig, scratch and scrape. He fought thorns, thistles and broccoli (whoops). Now he listened after nine months to the painful screams of Eve as children were born. What a shame. After all, it was only one rule. He couldn't claim, "I forgot." All he had was the simple Word of God, but he failed. We have followed his example ever since.

But God did not forget him. Eden provided an excellent picture of grace and the promises of God provided a grace-filled future.

Chapter 2

Noah Booms and Busts

Noah deserves the hall of fame of biblical characters, yet.... What incredible faith to build a boat far from the ocean on the promise of some strange never-before-seen phenomenon called *rain*. We would lock him up in our day, unless, of course, he was simply a rich or famous eccentric. What jesting he endured from his neighbors and tourists. What pain that no one would listen. What energy expended in rounding up two of each animal. What a bittersweet moment. As the rain fell, he gathered his family (who offered nothing to deserve this favor). God shut the door and Noah watched the obliteration of the human race except for those in his boat.

So much symbolism of redemption rides in the story of Noah and the ark right down to the moment when, in hope, he sent out a dove and it returned with an olive leaf in its mouth. But most of all, the human race had another chance.

Something happened to Noah in the interim. We can only speculate. Perhaps the need for a break after more than 100 years of ridicule and boat building and animal gathering. Perhaps five months of tending animals not known for hygiene. Perhaps being more than six hundred years old. Perhaps just being human. After leaving the ark, Noah built an altar, heard from God, then planted a vineyard. Soon he was lay-down drunk and as naked as if he were back in the garden. Out of this stupor mixed with an incestuous moment came the curse of Canaan.

Now ruined, our hero proves his ultimate incompetence. Yet through it all, we see the grace of God—the fact that Noah received God's grace to do the project, the fact that God gave the rainbow promise not to flood the earth again, and the fact that Noah continued to believe in and talk to God.

Chapter 3

Father Abraham Had Many Sons...

Abraham, the hero of billions, had two things going for him: the grace of God and his belief in God. His mal-treatment of his wife and disobedient actions, in re-sponse to the call and covenant of God, should remove him from all hero lists, yet *"Abraham believed God, and it was credited to him as righteousness,"* (James 2:23). *Good for Abraham.* Were it not for his *disbelief* later, Ishmael would not have been born and the tensions of this current world would be vastly different.

There Was a Crooked Man...

No one could be more blessed. A likely moon wor-shiper who hears an undeserved call from God and re-ceives the most incredible promise in a covenant from God.

> Get out of your country,
>
> From your family
>
> And from your father's house,
>
> To a land that I will show you.
>
> I will make you a great nation;

I will bless you

And make your name great;

And you shall be a blessing.

I will bless those who bless you,

And I will curse him who curses you;

And in you all the families of the earth shall be blessed.

Genesis 12:1-3 NKJ

Here, we receive a clear indication of the line of the Messiah, "…in you all the families of the earth shall be blessed." This pronouncement brings hope and amazement. Jesus was the only person of history who could choose his ancestry. Human logic demands that he choose outstanding individuals with exemplary holiness; however, no such persons seemed to be available. God had to work with incompetents like me, and you and Abraham.

Let us examine that messianic line from four positions: **Human Tradition**, **Logic**, **Hollywood** and **Heaven**.

Look at Abraham first. His first son, Ishmael, conceived out of impatience, should be the line-bearer according to the human tradition of birthright. According to logic, since birth by handmaiden was considered family, it should be Ishmael. According to Hollywood, the desert-dwelling Ishmael would delight screen-writers who glorify survival. According to Heaven, Isaac, yet to be born, was the one.

Indeed, the promise of a son as Abraham and Sarah neared 100 years of age brought about laughter, which is why they named him Isaac (the sound of laughter). Were he born in America, his name would be *ha ha*. However, God called Isaac Abraham's *only* son. Immediately, we see that God is not subject to human logic or traditions. We also note throughout Abraham's life with its moments of significant weakness, God continued to give and renew promises.

We also note that Abraham's family problems were of *biblical proportions*. Whenever newscasters/reporters want to describe some awesome moment, perhaps tragedy, they describe it with the term *biblical proportions*.

Isaac

Isaac's life offers little to commend him. He wasn't even able to find his own wife. Abraham, observing the aging Isaac, intervened to seek a wife by sending his servant (although don't miss the beautiful symbolism of the Holy Spirit seeking a bride for Christ and the bride, Rebekah, showing herself a true servant in watering the servant's camels). Like Sarah (Isaac's mother), Rebekah, his wife, turned up barren and only out of Isaac's prayer and God's mercy did she conceive.

Double Trouble

Twins are difficult enough to handle, but when they fight in the womb, you know you have a problem of major (biblical?) proportions. So Rebekah (not Isaac?) inquired of the Lord and the promise came that she had two nations in her womb and that the elder would serve the younger. Indeed, when Esau was born first, the other, still in the womb, reached out his arm and grabbed the heel of Esau as if to say, "Come back here. I am not through with this fight!" Consequently, the second born was named Jacob, heel catcher, which loosely translated means *Dirty Sneaky Thief.*

What a name to grow up with. You go to school and they call the roll, "Dirty Sneaky Thief?"

"Here."

You grow up and go to the bank to get a loan to go into business. "And your name, sir?"

"Dirty Sneaky Thief."

"Oh!"

Later, we see Jacob living up to his name. Meanwhile, Esau was a man's man. A hunter, an NRA member, hairy, an NFL lineman, a survivor(!), a body builder, a California governor, a twenty-game-winner, a hall-of-famer, a stinker, a dad's favorite.

On the other hand, Jacob was a paleface, a smoothie, a homebody, a kitchen dweller, a decorator, a mother's favorite, but still a *Dirty Sneaky Thief*. Catching Esau in a moment of great hunger, Jacob bought the birthright (a favored position which was Esau's by custom) for a bowl of stew. Now, Esau, despising his heritage, becomes a dirtbag equal to the Dirty Sneaky Thief who made the stew.

Trickery All Around

Obviously, Jacob and his mother assumed that the birthright bound God to Esau, and that Isaac's blessing of Esau might eliminate Jacob. Ah, our thoughts are so earthbound. God's thoughts soar infinitely higher than ours. No human mistake eliminates or deters God.

Isaac, nearing death and far in spirit from the promises of God, prepares to give the *official* blessing to his favorite, Esau, as soon as he returns from the hunt. That hunt was planned by Esau to provide a meal especially for Isaac to celebrate the bestowing of the "Messianic Blessing."

This cooked-up scheme reveals a flaw in the character of Isaac similar to that of Esau—an eternal heritage was about to sell cheap. Disobedience to the Word of God approached the doorstep as Isaac prepared to give the blessing to Esau and thus violate God's instruction that Jacob should prevail.

Rebekah, sister of Laban (ah, what we will learn about him!), and mother of Dirty Sneaky Thief, contrives to deceive Isaac and succeeds. Isaac thinks the well-disguised Jacob is Esau! Jacob gets the blessing (which was due him according to God, but didn't need deception to produce it). Esau is furious; Jacob runs for his life. Along the way, with a rock for a pillow, he has the famous dream of a ladder reaching to Heaven with angels traversing up and down.

There at the place he named Bethel (House of God) Jacob discovered that God's grace comes even to Dirty Sneaky Thief. Even incompetents cannot escape his loving care.

As for the line of the Messiah?

Logic says Esau.
Human tradition says Esau.
Hollywood declares Esau a super hero.
Heaven says Jacob.

Chapter 4

Jacob

Jacob's escape finally brought him to the land of his uncle, Laban. At a well where shepherds gathered to water their sheep, he met Rachel, daughter of his uncle, Laban. Ah, love at first sight.

Hollywood loves this kind of scene—a man of promise, but nothing in hand, meets beautiful woman, works hard for beautiful woman, loses beautiful woman, regains beautiful woman. After meeting Laban, Jacob asked for Rachel's hand. Laban said, "Wonderful. Love to have you as a son-in-law. All you need to do is work for me for seven years for her to be your wife." Jacob, blinded by love, failed to detect that he had met his match in sneakiness.

Joyous expectancy made the seven years seem like days. Oh, Rachel, Rachel! Wedding Day! Now, folks, the wedding tent lacked light switches so familiar to our day. At best, one or two candles barely held back the darkness. The bride's veil eliminated the faint light. Jacob entered that darkness for a joyful wedding night.

Light, the great revealer, broke into the tent and ignited the atmosphere. "Leah! Leah! What are you doing here? I wanted Rachel! Laban, what have you done to me?"

Trick Wife and Trophy Wife

"Oh, Jacob, didn't you know that the elder sister must marry before the younger one? So sorry. However, you can still have Rachel. Only seven more years of work."

Laban knew this was Leah's only hope. The name *Leah* means *wild cow* and *weary*. *Wild cow* is an oxymoron—mutually exclusive terms. Cows have always been domesticated. Perhaps Laban was saying "You're impossible." Additionally, he might have been saying, "You weary me." We know one other thing about Leah—she had *weak eyes*. Perhaps her squinting decreased what little attractiveness she might have had. The implication of the description indicates that looking at her would give you weak eyes. But now, she is married and married to someone who does not love her or want her and given by a father who does not love her or want her.

So! The deceiver got deceived. Further, the plot thickens. Leah, for all that she might lack, brought the greatest dowry, the most valued in that day—she bore Jacob one son right after another—Reuben, Simeon, Levi, Judah.... Rachel? Well, she was barren. We have come to a family problem of major (biblical) proportions. As for Jacob, he still didn't love Leah. In his mind, since Rachel was barren, he had no sons.

At this point, we pause and make some judgments about the line of the Messiah:

Logic: Reuben is the firstborn.

Human tradition: Reuben holds the birthright.

Hollywood: Rachel! Oh Rachel, please!!

Heaven: Unannounced.

If nothing else, the walk of Abraham, Isaac and Jacob proves that God works with the mentally and spiritually crippled.

The Runner Runs Again

Finally, after Leah had borne six sons, in Jacob's old age Rachel bore Joseph. To an ecstatic Jacob! To Jacob, he now had a son, his only son, Joseph. This favoritism later costs Jacob dearly.

However, now we make another judgment about the line of the Messiah:

Logic: Joseph.

Human tradition: Reuben.

Hollywood: Joseph, the dreamer.

Heaven: Still watching.

God prospered Laban because of Jacob, and Laban showed his deceitful nature throughout the relationship. Finally after twenty years of mutual deception, Laban invited Jacob to leave. Jacob agreed and managed to take with him the best portion of Laban's goods. His wife, Rachel, who had learned from both her father and her husband, managed to escape with the most valuable items in her father's house.

God had told Jacob to go home and he would bless him. Though Jacob attempted to bargain with God, he offered no further word. The problem? Home was where Esau lived and he might still be waiting to kill Jacob.

On the road, Laban chased Jacob's troop to rescue the family idols that Rachel had cleverly concealed. When he didn't find them, he set up some stones and called it *Mizpah* with this declaration, *"May the LORD watch between you and me when we are absent one from another."* (Genesis 31:49 NKJ) Many people end letters with that word *Mizpah* as an intended blessing for the reader. Ah, but not so! What Laban was saying was "God will be the policeman to watch you, you dirty sneaky thief, while I am not here to watch you." If you receive that blessing, you might want to seek clarification.

For once, Jacob tried diplomacy. He sent greetings and the offer of gifts to Esau, but then learned that Esau with an army of 400 men marched toward them. The end had come.

Sometimes, in crisis, we easily forget the promises of God. Jacob did. Though he reminded God of those promises, he did not act out of them. Now, he could run no more. The Mizpah agreement prohibited his return to Laban. Obviously, Esau intended to exact his vengeance on Jacob. He had nowhere to run. It was over.

Jacob took defensive measures. He divided his company into two groups and sent them in opposite directions. After his first dark night, he sent large gifts over to Esau. Then, in his final defensive act, the Bible records: *And he arose that night and took his two wives, his two female servants, and his eleven sons, and crossed over the ford of Jabbok. He took them, sent them over the brook, and sent over what he had.* [Then] *Jacob was left alone;...* (Genesis 32:22-24)

And in This Corner...

Jacob, alone! No one to share this final moment. No one to encourage him. He knew this was his last night alive. He knew he had seen his family for the last time. As one song lyric declared, "One is the loneliest number." Perhaps the most difficult part is that he was alone with *himself*. What a thing to be alone with when your name is *Dirty Sneaky Thief*.

But *one* in God's plan is never alone. In the briefest of descriptions, the Bible puts it this way: "and a Man wrestled with him until the breaking of day." Later, we discover that this is a pre-fleshly appearance of Jesus. Now, in your mind's eye, how does Jesus look to you? Does he look like the handsome, Irish, Salman's Head of Christ? In your mind's eye, what does a wrestler look like? Can you imagine Jesus looking like that?

Whatever you imagine, we have two men wrestling *all night long*. I have watched college and Olympic wrestling matches. If they last the maximum of perhaps nine minutes, the wrestlers spend the next thirty minutes lying in exhaustion. But all night? There was something in this kitchen boy Jacob we missed. This is the sort of match tailor-made for someone like Esau, not Jacob. When it came to wrestling with God, he was *good*. In fact, God whipped Jacob's hip out of socket to equalize the match. Jacob, unfazed, kept going. Remember, too, that Jacob was now an old man.

Then Jacob made one of the best decisions of his life. He surrendered. When God saw that this match was a draw, he said, *"Let me go, for the day breaks."* But he (Jacob) said, *"I will not let you go unless you bless me!"* (Genesis 32:22-32 NKJ)

In case you wonder how this was surrender, here is the explanation. In very old days, the winner (who was stronger) would give a gift (a show of strength) to the loser (who in weakness received it). Sometimes kings would battle by gift-giving. The king giving the greater gift sent the lesser king home in shame. So, if you were a wrestler in that day, a trophy case filled with trophies merely advertised your incompetence.

So, Jacob was saying, "I lose, you win, and you must not leave here until you accept your victory and give me a gift." Brilliant! He recognized who he was wrestling with. So God said to him, *"What is your name?"* He said, *"Jacob."*

Why that question? Surely his name plagued him. Reality settled on Jacob. He may be the best wrestler in the world. He may even be in the dirty sneaky thief hall of fame, but he was still a dirty sneaky thief. Even in this day, we know that those who run away to start a new life carry a fatal poison—themselves. This was his ultimate shame, to have to admit to God that his name was accurate, but it was his greatest victory. Even in this day, when we dirty sneaky thieves finally admit the truth to God, we reach our greatest victory.

Ah, but what a trophy Jacob received. And God said, *"Your name shall no longer be called Jacob, but Israel; for you have struggled with God and with men, and have prevailed."* (Genesis 32:28 NKJ)

Wait, wait! I just surrendered and you are declaring me the winner? *Yes.* Let's go through this again.... Israel! *He struggles with God.* Israel! *Prince of God.* God had kissed this frog and turned him into a prince just as he does to us spiritual frogs to this day. If ever we see the grace and mercy of God, we see it in this moment. *And Jacob called the name of the place Peniel: 'For I have seen God face to face, and my life is preserved.'* (Genesis 32:30 NKJ)

You Can't Hit a Cripple

Yes, Israel is now a prince, but he is a crippled prince. Then, as dawn came, he saw Esau coming with his 400 men. Israel limped toward Esau, and Esau fell on his neck and kissed him and wept. His life was saved. But now, in his relationship with Esau, Israel shows the old spirit of Jacob as his deception returns. Fascinating! Indeed, later God would refer to himself as the God of Abraham, Isaac and *Dirty Sneaky Thief*. Folks, that is grace and mercy.

At this point, Jacob had eleven sons, then, at his great age, Rachel gave birth to her second and Jacob's last son and, as she did, breathed her last. Rachel wanted to name him Ben-oni, son of my sorrow, but Jacob named him Benjamin, son of my right hand, or son of my strength—a bit of advertising here for an old man.

So here is a man with major family and personal problems to the degree that we call them of *biblical proportions*. Do you ever wonder why God chose and used Jacob? Maybe this is part of the plan of God to use the unusable, save the unsaveable, accept the rejected. The glory goes only to God.

Chapter 5

Joseph, The Favorite Son

> Now Israel loved Joseph more than all his
> children, because he was the son of his old
> age. Also he made him a tunic of many
> colors. But when his brothers saw that their
> father loved him more than all his brothers,
> they hated him and could not speak peacea-
> bly to him.
>
> Genesis 37:3-4 NKJ

Dinner table conversation at the house of Jacob
seethed with hatred. I can hear the bitterness of the sons
of Leah and Zilpah and Bilhah: "Why doesn't Dad love
my mother? What did you accomplish to become his favorite? You haven't done a day's work in your life, Joseph. Why the fancy clothes for you? You will never get
those dirty. Your only job is tattling on us and having
obnoxious dreams."

You must admit, Jacob's favoritism made a spoiled
brat of Joseph. I find it difficult to regard this favoritism
of Jacob as a righteous act. Whenever a family chooses a
favorite, they create family dysfunction of (here we go
again) *biblical proportions.*

When Joseph related his dream of their (his brothers)
sheaves bowing down to his own and then relating the

dream of the sun and moon (his parents) bowing down to his star, the situation only worsened. Some very personal promises from God are not necessarily to be communicated to others; but if you are spoiled, wisdom may be lacking. I find it difficult to consider this a righteous action on the part of Joseph. Amazing, though, how adversity makes you grow. Amazing, how much adversity came to Joseph.

The brothers captured Joseph on a tattle-tale mission. They first conspired to kill him, but Reuben intervened to save his life and planned to return him to Jacob. They put him in a pit. Plans advanced to rip the beautiful coat and soak it with blood to fool Jacob. Judah, unwilling to murder his own flesh, lobbied the brothers to instead sell Joseph to Ishmaelites traveling to Egypt.

At this point, we turn toward another judgment about the line of the Messiah:

Human tradition: Reuben.
Logic: Reuben.
Hollywood: Reeling over the loss of Rachel.
Heaven: Jury still out.

The Temptress

Joseph, bought by a man named Potiphar, achieves prosperity with consequent high responsibility. Now, in charge of all Potiphar's possessions, a major problem surfaces: Potiphar's wife falls for Joseph's good looks.

Meantime, back home in a sordid tale, Judah visits a prostitute not knowing it was a setup by the widow of his son (whom he had not treated properly according to tradition). She, the widow of his son, ended up having twins, one of them named Perez, part of the Messianic line. Amazing.

But, back to Joseph. Day after day, Potiphar's wife attempted to seduce Joseph. He resisted, probably knowing resistance had a high price tag; however, greater wisdom would have brought Joseph into a discussion with Potiphar about the situation, even though that act could be costly as well.

Apparently, that did not happen. Perhaps Joseph was enjoying the temptation too much. I see a lack of righteousness in this situation in spite of the outcome. Ultimately, her attempts and his resistance landed him in prison in a false accusation. Perhaps he began to seriously question his dreams. However, we do know that previously with his brothers, he pled for his life. Doubts must have swept across his soul frequently.

Demotion

Jail time increased his dependence on God and instigated God's action in his life. Finally, his interpretation of Pharaoh's dream brought him into an incredible position of power. God exhibited his mercy—certain proof that God uses the weak and the foolish.

God's mercy gave Joseph power while in prison, but that power failed to save him from great disappointment. Joseph interpreted positively the dream of the king's butler who was also in prison. Joseph asked the butler to remember him when he was in the castle, but the butler instead quickly erased his memories of prison. Tough!

Finally, Pharaoh himself had a dream that none of his wise men could interpret. Aha! Then the butler remembered! Joseph's interpretation of Pharaoh's dream opened the door to unequaled prominence—all the while giving glory to God.

Little noticed in this story is a loss of opportunity by Joseph. In his position, rather than proclaim the power of the God of all creation, Joseph affirmed the state religion. He protected the ownership of land by the state religion and the priests. Joseph even married the daughter of a pagan priest. Perhaps it was political expediency.

(I suffer constant disillusionment from those who run on the platform of Jesus in politics, but fail to act out of the nature of Jesus when elected. Politics always wins.)

Joseph Gets His Revenge

Now, though, we jump forward to the height of the predicted famine, a famine that reached into the land of Jacob, where the news had arrived that there was food in Egypt. The ten brothers (Leah's and her handmaiden's sons only) are sent to buy food. Ignorant that Joseph led the food distribution, they were caught by the fact that they were recognized by Joseph. There begins a series of games designed to humiliate the brothers and bring further grief to Jacob. Immediate revelation by Joseph would have terrified the brothers and, in fear of their lives, would have brought about the repentance that they later exhibited. Such a move would have been kind to his father, Jacob. I find it difficult to consider Joseph's manipulation of his brothers as righteousness.

Further, in the course of this mishandling, Joseph lies to the brothers claiming that he can *divine in the cup* (a form of sorcery), the very kind of divination that God condemns. None-the-less, we reach a vital moment in the final scheme of Joseph. He manipulated the brothers into bringing Benjamin down to Egypt.

Jacob feared the worst, but Reuben promised that if they didn't bring Benjamin back, Jacob could kill Reuben's two sons as retribution. Now, that is quite a sacrifice; however, we don't know what his two sons were like. Maybe Reuben would have considered that a great convenience.

Regardless, we have reached another judgment point from this offer of Reuben in the line of Christ.

Logic: Reuben.

Human tradition: Reuben, the firstborn.

Hollywood: Forget it. Let's do an investigation.

Heaven: Still uncommitted, but we have a clue.

A Star Is Born

Sure enough, when they arrived in Egypt with Benjamin, Joseph manipulated the situation so that he could keep Benjamin in jail. At that point a most remarkable thing happens. Judah steps up and pleads his case and offers an ultimate deal:

> "Then your servant my father said to us, 'You know that my wife bore me two sons; and the one went out from me, and I said, "Surely he is torn to pieces"; and I have not seen him since. But if you take this one also from me, and calamity befalls him, you shall bring down my gray hair with sorrow to the grave.'
>
> "Now therefore, when I come to your servant my father, and the lad is not with us, since his life is bound up in the lad's life, it will happen, when he sees that the lad is not with us, that he will die. So your servants will

bring down the gray hair of your servant our father with sorrow to the grave.

"For your servant became surety for the lad to my father, saying, 'If I do not bring him back to you, then I shall bear the blame before my father forever.'

"Now therefore, please let your servant remain instead of the lad as a slave to my lord, and let the lad go up with his brothers. For how shall I go up to my father if the lad is not with me, lest perhaps I see the evil that would come upon my father?"

Genesis 44:27-34 NKJ

Judah, son number four of Leah, pleads with Joseph that he be permitted to take the place of Benjamin basically declaring " If you must enslave someone, let me be the one. If someone is to die, let me die in his place."

My heart leaps within me. Here, Judah exhibits the spirit most like Jesus himself. Here, he rises above all his brothers in understanding, even to accepting the fact that Jacob's life was totally wrapped up in the half-brother, named Benjamin, even to accepting the fact that Jacob considered only Rachel as his wife and mother of his children.

I can almost hear the thunder as the flame of God streaks through the universe to write indelibly in the pages of history, in the genetics of hope, that the line was now established.

Now we can make the final judgment with the help of an additional verse:

> Now the sons of Reuben the firstborn of Israel—he was indeed the firstborn, but because he defiled his father's bed, his birthright was given to the sons of Joseph, the son of Israel, so that the genealogy is not listed according to the birthright; yet Judah prevailed over his brothers, and from him came a ruler, although the birthright was Joseph's.... 1 Chronicles 5:1–3 NKJ

Logic: Reuben.
Human tradition: Joseph.
Hollywood: Who can we get to do Moses?
Heaven: Judah.
Jesus will be the Lion of the tribe of Judah.

Also, Jacob, as he approaches his death, finally obeys the will of God, as he voices prophecies concerning each of his sons, accurately describing the office of Judah, the fourth son of the wife he did not love:

> Judah, you are he whom your brothers shall praise; your hand shall be on the neck of your enemies; your father's children shall bow down before you.
>
> Judah is a lion's whelp; from the prey, my son, you have gone up. He bows down, he

lies down as a lion; and as a lion, who shall rouse him?

The scepter shall not depart from Judah, nor a lawgiver from between his feet, until Shiloh comes; and to him shall be the obedience of the people.

Binding his donkey to the vine, and his donkey's colt to the choice vine, he washed his garments in wine, and his clothes in the blood of grapes.

His eyes are darker than wine, and his teeth whiter than milk.

Genesis 49:8–12 NKJ

We learn much from this narrative:

1. God obviously uses the weak and foolish. Indeed, he can't use us until we are weak and foolish.

2. You find the *Nature of Jesus* throughout the Bible if you simply look. The Old Testament points forward to Jesus. The New Testament points back to him. He is the central focus of eternity.

3. God is not bound by human tradition or logic or Hollywood.

4. God can accomplish his purposes without our intervention or panic.

5. To God, everyone is beautiful.

True Love Equals Beauty

I can hear God whispering to Leah, "I know your father did not love you and gave you a name that was an insult. I know that your husband didn't love you and received you under protest. I know that to the world you are not beautiful. But, Leah, I think you are beautiful. Your name is sweet to me. In fact, I would like for you to be one of my mothers."

Years ago, as my son, Clyde, and I were driving together in a mountainous area, we rounded a corner and exclaimed in awe at the beauty of a valley scene below us. I told him that this is a disproof of evolution, since the fact that this is beautiful to us has no evolutionary benefit. The question of beauty tweaked my son's thinking. I shall never forget his response. "Dad, I think humanity's view of beauty is a result of the fall of mankind. After the fall, we began to separate people into the beautiful and the ugly, but, to God, everyone is beautiful."

One thing I observe: All women feel that they are not beautiful enough. The exorbitant amount of money spent on creams and soaps and oils is proof. Even the women considered by the world as the most beautiful still apply a world of makeup simply because they feel they are not beautiful enough. But please hear me when I say this: That is the view of sinful mankind. To God, you are beautiful.

Chapter 6

Joseph's Surprising Command

Joseph brings his family down to Egypt to enjoy the fruit of his position. Border crossings are always a pain, but this should not be any trouble for the family of the man who was only a half step below Pharaoh. All they have to do is say, "Uh, Joseph is my brother." Immediate entry would be guaranteed. However, Joseph issues a strange command to his family:

> "So it shall be, when Pharaoh calls you and says, 'What is your occupation?' that you shall say, 'Your servants' occupation has been with livestock from our youth even till now, both we and also our fathers,' that you may dwell in the land of Goshen; for every shepherd is an abomination to the Egyptians."
> Genesis 46:33-34 NKJ

Wait! Wait! Joseph says, in essence, "Tell them the truth. Tell them you are shepherds, because Egyptians despise shepherds!" How different from the normal! Rather than let them drink from the cup of power, he tells them to choose the despised way.

Consider, also, that when Jacob relegated the sons of Leah to the shepherd fields, he was making a statement about how he viewed these sons—the lowest. Joseph and Benjamin never had to touch a sheep.

This sounds remarkably like the very nature of Jesus when he made himself of *no reputation* as Paul relates in Philippians 2:7. It sounds like Jesus saying to his disciples, *"I send you out as lambs among wolves."* (Luke 10:3 NKJ) What would be the benefit of such humility? Very simple. Since Egyptians held such a vocation in contempt, they considered them no threat to their country or economy; consequently, they gave them the best land of Egypt, the land of Goshen. Sounds remarkably like another command of Scripture: "Humble yourselves in the sight of the Lord, and he shall lift you up." (James 4:10 KJV)

Again, we see that the despised, the incompetent, the failed, the misfit, the outcast—all match the requirements of God to be used and blessed.

Chapter 7

Moses, from Boss to Baaa

Israel, as a nation, progressed from famine to fame to prosperity to slavery. Enter, the grace and mercy of God. Moses, by divine intervention, became a son of Pharaoh, probably destined for the throne. He earned a PhD in Egyptology, but his roots extended into the slave camp of Israelis. Though Scripture doesn't indicate, he must have been a man of strong physique because he saw an Egyptian mistreating an Israeli; and he killed him single-handedly.

Ah, power corrupts and the powerful begin to feel they can get away with anything. Perhaps they can in much of the world, but God is never fooled, nor does he ever need our intervention to achieve his plan. Now, Moses, a prince, a man of sophistication, educated to the limit, privileged at the highest level, heir apparent to the throne, destined deliverer of Israel, ran for his life. He really ran. All the way to the far side of the desert where he worked as a shepherd and married the daughter of Jethro (also called Reuel) a Midianite. Little did he know that the Midianites would later become a major enemy of Israel.

Perhaps we should understand shepherds better in order to see what had happened to Moses. True, the Egyptians despised shepherds, but they were not alone in this cultural practice. Note the disposition of David when Samuel came to anoint a son of Jesse as king. Jesse withheld David from the beauty contest provided for the benefit of Samuel because David was a shepherd. At least, that is one reason.

In the time of Jesus, shepherds were considered the lowest life-form on the face of the earth. Pharisees believed that a shepherd could not get forgiveness for his sins because he had committed so many. No one would trust a shepherd. They were like your local burglars. When they went through town, things tended to disappear. To this very day in the Middle East, shepherds remain lowest in status with no means or ability to rise.

So, Moses went from the very top to the very lowest and not as a temporary position. This new job lasted forty years. Listen to how he viewed himself at the beginning and at the end of that time:

At the beginning: Acts 7:22

> Moses was educated in all the wisdom of the Egyptians and was powerful in speech and action.

At the end: Exodus 3:11

> But Moses said to God, "Who am I, that I should go to Pharaoh and bring the Israelites out of Egypt?"

Exodus 4:1

> Moses answered, "What if they do not believe me or listen to me and say, 'The LORD did not appear to you'?"

Exodus 4:10

> Moses said to the LORD, "O Lord, I have never been eloquent, neither in the past nor since you have spoken to your servant. I am slow of speech and tongue."

Exodus 4:13

> But Moses said, "O Lord, please send someone else to do it."

When he finished his journey from the *mighty* to the *weak and foolish*, he stood in the place of usability. In finally becoming the meekest man on the earth, he occupied a place of future triumph when the prophecy came: *"This is that Moses who told the Israelites, 'God will send you a prophet like me from your own people.'"* (Acts 7:37)

Once again we see our heroes rising to the ranks of *not many mighty* where God begins to show his might.

Chapter 8

Gideon, the Lowest of the Low

That period between the wilderness wanderings and the first king of Israel, commonly known as the time of the judges, lasted hundreds of years. Though filled with the magnificent and the miserable, one very miserable time brings us to a reluctant hero.

The Midianites, who dominated Israel for years, were smart. They left Israel alone to plant and bring in their crops. Then when they saw them up on the hilltop threshing floors (threshing floors needed to be where the wind would blow), the Midianites would determine the appropriate time and go take the crop.

We join our hero, not on the hilltop, but hidden down in a wine press (out of the wind because you didn't want the wind blowing debris into the brew) where he threshed his harvest. Ah, but this made the work much more difficult. He had to throw the grain up and then blow on it himself to separate the chaff. Here, Gideon encountered God.

> Gideon was threshing wheat in a winepress to keep it from the Midianites. When the angel of the LORD appeared to

Gideon, he said, "The LORD is with you, mighty warrior."

"But sir," Gideon replied, "if the LORD is with us, why has all this happened to us? Where are all his wonders that our fathers told us about when they said, 'Did not the LORD bring us up out of Egypt?' But now the LORD has abandoned us and put us into the hand of Midian."

The LORD turned to him and said, "Go in the strength you have and save Israel out of Midian's hand. Am I not sending you?"

"But Lord," Gideon asked, "how can I save Israel? My clan is the weakest in Manasseh, and I am the least in my family."
Judges 6:11-15

Interesting, isn't it, that God chose the lowest member of the lowest family of Manasseh to accomplish a great deliverance. Here we are with the *non-noble* again. Gideon believed God and, after a moment of doubt that originated what we call *putting out a fleece*, he blew the shofar, (ram's horn) that mobilized Israel and 32,000 men showed up.

Gideon looked at his troops and looked across the valley at 120,000 Midianite soldiers. He probably looked back and forth several times. Put yourself in the shoes of Gideon. What are you going to pray for? Obviously, "God, I need another 100,000 men!" But I

38

can hear God saying, "Gideon, you have too many men." If I were Gideon, I would have asked for a second opinion. Perhaps he did. If so, I can hear God saying, "Gideon, you have *way* too many men. Send the scared ones home."

The Diminishing Army

Gideon obeyed, told the scared ones to go home and 22,000 men left. Ouch. This can affect his prayer life. Last time he prayed, it cost him 22,000 men. What will happen now? Well, God informed him that he still had too many men—give them a further test, have them take a drink of water. I'm sure Gideon thought, "God, sometimes you are pretty hard to work for." Now, we seldom consider a drink of water to be a test and this one surprises us:

> "Every one that lappeth of the water with his tongue, as a dog lappeth, him shalt thou set by himself; likewise every one that boweth down upon his knees to drink."

> And the number of them that lapped, putting their hand to their mouth, were three hundred men: but all the rest of the people bowed down upon their knees to drink water.

And the LORD said unto Gideon, "By
the three hundred men that lapped will I
save you."
Judges 7:5-7 KJV

So those who got down on all fours to drink straight
into their mouths were put on one side and those who
scooped the water with their hands were put on another
side. Gideon looked and knew—9,700 men arose from
lapping and only 300 arose from scooping. As a man
who grew up in church, I have always heard that these
300 were the elite warriors who knew how to drink and,
at the same time, stay alert. I no longer believe that.

First, Israel didn't have 300 elite warriors. Second,
God was reducing the army to the ones who would give
him the glory, to the ones who would not say his own
hand had saved Israel. Third, nothing in the story indicates that these men were elite warriors. When Gideon
gave them instructions, he placed a shofar in one hand
and a jug with a torch in the other hand. What? No
sword? When they were instructed to break the jugs to
reveal the torches and then blow the trumpets, they then
simply stood there. No rushing toward the enemy.

Consequently, I am now convinced that these 300
were men too fat or too crippled to get down on all fours
to drink. These men, if the battle is won, can give only
God the glory. If we win, believe me, God gets the glory.
The kingdom of *not many mighty* marches on.

Chapter 9

Samson, Blinded by a Woman

It was the worst of times. The Philistines had ruled and ruined Israel for 40 years—actually as judgment for their sheer paganism. Then God told a man named Manoah and his wife they would have a son who must never drink wine nor eat unclean food nor have his hair cut—the covenant of a Nazirite.

> The woman gave birth to a boy and named him Samson. He grew and the LORD blessed him,...
> Judges 13:24

Although he was a judge, he had a serious weakness—women. Now, one would think that God would make fornication part of the Nazirite vow, even so, such a prohibition should be understood from the Law. Regardless, God blessed this man and used him. One wonders what Samson might have accomplished had he been a faithful, godly man. But still we marvel:

> ...and the Spirit of the LORD began to stir him...
> Judges 13:25

However, the fame of Samson rests in his strength, phenomenal strength that cost the Philistines thousands of lives and harvests of crops. Whenever Hollywood attempts to create films about this man, he is always shown as a world-class body-builder type of person. This is so opposite to the evidence of the Bible. Samson even marries a Philistine, Delilah; and she, manipulated by the Philistines, sought to determine the secret of Samson's strength.

Had Samson been muscular, they would have known the source of his strength, so he must not have been. Who would ever have guessed that the secret was his hair? Actually, the Holy Spirit provided his strength. The hair merely signaled obedience to his vows.

So, what physical appearance of Samson caused Delilah to wonder at the source of his strength? Let me propose an option. Perhaps he was short, fat and wore suspenders. (um, kaf) And when Delilah finished with him, he was probably short, fat and *bald* and wore suspenders—like me. (um, kaf, kaf)

At any rate, further evidence that God leans toward the incompetent.

Chapter 10

Balaam, a Donkey of a Man

If one hunts for the most unusable, greedy character in the Bible, he need look no further than a prophet named Balaam. Why God chose to use a greedy, seedy sorcerer to make some of the greatest prophecies about Israel and the Messiah escapes me.

Here, a famous man, whose donkey, smarter and more spiritual than he, and who, humorously in my opinion, carried on a conversation with his donkey, failed to see the armed and dangerous angel blocking his greedy path. Even more humorously, the angel said that though he would have killed Balaam had he continued, he would have spared the donkey. Balaam relentlessly looked for some way to receive the gifts from Balak, the ruler of Moab. Balak wanted to pay Balaam for cursing Israel, but God allowed Balaam to prophecy only blessing. However, in the end, for a fee, Balaam told Balak how to corrupt Israel through idolatry and immorality.

I am staggered that this *dumber than a donkey* guy would issue the following prophecies. It proves that God can use the loser and rescue the incompetent. However, the Scriptures following from The New Testament show that Balaam's fame flows not from the prophecies but from his unrighteous greed.

"Arise, Balak, and listen; hear me, son of Zippor. God is not a man, that he should lie, nor a son of man, that he should change his mind. Does he speak and then not act? Does he promise and not fulfill? I have received a command to bless; he has blessed, and I cannot change it.

"No misfortune is seen in Jacob, no misery observed in Israel. The LORD their God is with them; the shout of the King is among them. God brought them out of Egypt; they have the strength of a wild ox. There is no sorcery against Jacob, no divination against Israel. It will now be said of Jacob and of Israel, 'See what God has done!' The people rise like a lioness; they rouse themselves like a lion that does not rest till he devours his prey and drinks the blood of his victims."
Numbers 23:18-24 24:9

"How beautiful are your tents, O Jacob, your dwelling places, O Israel!

"Like valleys they spread out, like gardens beside a river, like aloes planted by the LORD, like cedars beside the waters. Water will flow from their buckets; their seed will have abundant water.

"Their king will be greater than Agag; their kingdom will be exalted.

"God brought them out of Egypt; they have the strength of a wild ox. They devour hostile nations and break their bones in pieces; with their arrows they pierce them. Like a lion they crouch and lie down, like a lioness—who dares to rouse them?

"May those who bless you be blessed and those who curse you be cursed!"
Numbers 24:5-10

"I see him, but not now; I behold him, but not near. A star will come out of Jacob; a scepter will rise out of Israel. He will crush the foreheads of Moab, the skulls of all the sons of Sheth. Edom will be conquered; Seir, his enemy, will be conquered, but Israel will grow strong. A ruler will come out of Jacob and destroy the survivors of the city."
Numbers 24:17-19

Now, we see how the direction of Balaam's heart ruined him and affected a nation.

They have left the straight way and wandered off to follow the way of Balaam son of Beor, who loved the wages of wickedness. But he was rebuked for his wrongdoing by a donkey-a beast without speech-who spoke with a man's voice and restrained the prophet's madness.
2 Peter 2:15-16

Woe to them! They have taken the way of Cain; they have rushed for profit into Balaam's error; they have been destroyed in Korah's rebellion.

Jude 1:11

Nevertheless, I have a few things against you: You have people there who hold to the teaching of Balaam, who taught Balak to entice the Israelites to sin by eating food sacrificed to idols and by committing sexual immorality.

Revelation 2:14

Chapter 11

Elijah, Failure Follows Fire

> Elijah was a man just like us. He prayed earnestly that it would not rain, and it did not rain on the land for three and a half years.
>
> James 5:17

God speaks through the prophets to the *system* from outside the system—almost always. The role of the prophet stands out in Scripture much more than the role of the king in hearing from God. Why? Probably because the king, corrupted by his power, has nothing to say since in his business, he has little time to hear from God, indeed, has much needing to be said to him. The prophet, always coming from outside the power system (beltway?) hears clearly from God and speaks faithfully. How does the king respond? By killing prophets.

Jesus criticized the Pharisees intensely for not only killing the prophets but blatantly building memorial tombs for them. Such hypocrisy lives on today. Jerusalem, capitol city for the whole world of religion received the same criticism—*"You, who kill the prophets."*

Prophets emerge from powerless backgrounds. Such humble backgrounds embolden the corrupted powerful leaders to oppose and consequently kill the prophets rather than heed their warnings from God. Elijah fit the job description throughout his life. He is called Elijah the Tishbite. That means he was from the town or region of Tishba in Gilead. Where is Tishba? Though we are not absolutely sure, some scholars think that Tishba was a Gentile town.

Imagine that! God sends a despised Gentile to speak to nationalistic Israel. Then, to further lower his power standing, Elijah spent most of his life in hiding. Not even a chance for a press briefing. No television available to publish his propaganda. Even his aid knew he hated publicity and wanted encounters only to produce good results. We know so little, but we know that Ahab, the king of Israel, lived in terror at the thought of Elijah. He knew that the devastating drought hovered over his land because of the word of Elijah. Obadiah, servant to Ahab but still one of the good guys, told Elijah, "There is no nation or kingdom where my master has not sent someone to hunt for you."

Superbowl #1

Elijah agreed to meet Ahab and from that meeting called a great religious Super Bowl gathering on Mount Carmel. Jezebel, Ahab's queen had killed all of the prophets known in the land, so Elijah alone faced the 450 prophets of Baal in the great fireworks show. In that encounter God proves again that his greatest shows of power occur in the presence of human weakness. After the prophets of Baal performed every religious trick known to them and invoked every incantation while suffering the taunts of Elijah, finally, it was God's turn to use his exiled prophet. After insuring the inability to burn by pouring excessive water on the sacrifice, Elijah prayed the simplest of prayers—so unlike most public praying—that used no incantations or secret words or actions. The result? Fire!

After killing the 450 prophets of Baal, Elijah, brimming with spiritual adrenaline, predicts rain, then outruns the chariots to Jezreel so as not to be caught in the downpour. Then, Elijah, in fear (?) keeps on running, now terrified at the threat of Jezebel. Wait! Isn't this the great and brave prophet? What happened? He proved that he was just like I am—human. When the Bible records in James 5:17 that Elijah was a man of like passion (or human just like the rest of us), that is not a good recommendation. Nothing to put on your resume.

The Whisper

Finally, awakened by an angel after his run and sleep, Elijah goes to *The Cave* hoping to hear from God (as if he had not heard earlier). This cave occupies a sacred place in Jewish history. Whenever you say *The Wall* to a Jewish person, he only thinks of the Wailing Wall in Jerusalem. Whenever you say *The Cave,* you bring only this cave to mind—this cave that Moses first entered on top of Mt. Horeb and received the Ten Commandments as well as the definition of God's Name. The cave that symbolizes Jesus himself.

It would make sense to go there to hear from God, and Elijah expects a great show of force from a great God. Ah, but the wind, the earthquake and the fire fail him. Instead, in a *still small voice*, the kind of voice one can hear anywhere whether prophet or not, God speaks. Elijah appears again a few times, but the great super bowl appearance is over.

Does God abandon him? Is he any less in God's eyes because he is now less in the kingdom. Not at all. God prepares a huge *fiery chariot* to bring him into Heaven.

But the story does not end with a diminished Elijah. Again, not at all. God uses the *return* of Elijah to signal the coming of the Messiah. *"See, I will send you the prophet Elijah before that great and dreadful day of the LORD comes."* (Malachi 4:5)

What an awesome honor. Another honor awaited him, another very high honor. When Jesus climbed that mountain that we now call the Mount of Transfiguration, two people joined him there—Moses and Elijah, the two who sought to hear his voice in *The Cave*. Two men with great victories, but also great failures. Sounds like God's people.

Chapter 12

David

We remember and admire David because of his greatness as king, his prowess in battle, the designation of his line as that of the Messiah. Who can forget the triumph over Goliath? Even the secular world uses the David versus Goliath story. Jesus accepted the title "Son of David."

But we forget the humble and despised status of David when we first observe him. Jesse exhibited understandable pride as he marched his sons in front of Samuel, God's representative who watched and listened to hear which one would bear the crown. Indeed, Samuel observed the making of a king in each one of them. However, God said "No" to each of them. Samuel feared for his life, because God had commissioned him to find a king and he had failed. Understandable.

What was it about David that kept him out of the lineup? When *king* reached Jesse's ears, what trait eliminated David? He must have looked lesser than his brothers. Though he was *ruddy* he apparently lacked that *something* that said *king*. Perhaps his difference in looks actually embarrassed Jesse. Perhaps that difference created questions in minds, questions that he didn't want in the mind of Samuel.

David, relegated to the sheep herd, might not have known that a king contest was happening in his front yard. Being a shepherd does take some attention. Keep in mind that shepherd was the lowest of occupations, the lowest of status, the most despised, the least trusted. Shepherd was the one occupation that prohibited ambition and left an iron ceiling thwarting any rise in stature. Could David have been put out with the sheep as a form of punishment? We can only speculate. Whatever we think, we know that Jesse, his father, never thought of him as king.

Even as David entered the scene of a boasting, mocking Goliath, his brothers despised his presence. No one spotted, in his heart or genes, the making of a king or Messiah except the King of Kings and the Messiah himself.

David lived as a fugitive, surrounded by misfits and running for his life. The world of his day, as well as ours, celebrates his ability to kill tens of thousands; however, God celebrated David's love for him and worship of him, declaring him a man after his own heart, all this in spite of major moral failures.

So, God used David rather than his impressive brothers or the impressive King Saul, who started out in humility but ended in arrogance and disobedience. David kept a repentant heart, not always obedient, but always repentant. Perhaps God wants our hearts to stay in the field of sheep.

PART TWO

Flawed Apostles
Flawed Forerunner

For the message of the cross is
foolishness to those who are perishing,
but to us who are being saved it is the
power of God. For it is written:
"I will destroy the wisdom of the wise;
the intelligence of the intelligent I will
frustrate."
1 Corinthians 1:18–19

It is because of him that you are in
Christ Jesus, who has become for us
wisdom from God—that is, our
righteousness, holiness and redemption.
Therefore, as it is written: "Let him who
boasts boast in the Lord."
1 Corinthians 1:30–31

Chapter 13

Choosing Apostles

Leaders? What Leaders?

Jesus chose twelve men to be *with him* and called them apostles. The word *apostle* means *sent one*. Let us keep that definition in mind as we continue this study. Because they walked with Jesus, if for no other reason, we hold them in high regard ascribing to them all the traits we consider to be ideal—stature, voice, physique, face, etc. Perhaps that is a major error.

How did Jesus choose a cabinet? Had he just consulted with me, I could have helped him. My recommendations?

1. Go to the theological seminaries and choose several professors who understand the theological ramifications of the problems that arise.

2. Then go to Hollywood and get someone with charisma who can command the attention of the crowd and explain what you *meant* when you said such and such.

3. Then go to Wall Street and get several millionaires—they're nice to have on the team.

4. Then go to Muscle Beach and get about six body guards, because they will crucify you around here if you aren't careful.

But Jesus ignored my advice. Instead he chose men from the street, smelly fishermen, men with strong and revealing accents, a tax collector and a Zealot (natural enemies).

Note that Jesus prayed all night before he selected them. So, what did he get? The next pages relate a litany of shortcomings, outright failures, misunderstandings, ignorances, hostilities, misinterpretations, disobediences, misconceptions and power struggles.

But look at this brief list of Jesus' answers to prayer and see what he got. Well, he got one who denied him and another who betrayed him. Bad start. They all abandoned him at some point. They all got angry at him. They never seemed to understand what he was saying (we will discuss this later). They stopped someone from doing good because he didn't have a membership card. They rebuked mothers for bringing children to Jesus. They wanted to torch a village because they were not allowed to spend the night there (a new evangelistic program, I guess).

But their most frequent activity was simply arguing with each other. Of course, we think they argued about deep theological subjects. Not so! They argued constantly about which of them was the greatest.

Remember that these were the A-postles not the B-postles. This was the A-team. Or maybe the D-ciples.

And Jesus prayed all night before he chose them! Either he wasted the prayer, or else, that was what he prayed for. Maybe he prayed, "Father, don't let me choose the ones that high academics or big business would choose. Let me choose the ones who, when we use them, everyone will say, 'It was God!'"

The more we look without preconceptions at the apostles in the Gospels, the more we realize that Jesus chose a group that we would call *losers*. Keep in mind that he did not choose these men from the halls of academicia. Education of that day was religious schools for Torah study. Those who lacked the intelligence or motivation to achieve were released to *get a job*. So, where did Jesus find his men? At work! These men were somewhere down the ladder in terms of intelligence, though from frequenting the synagogues they would have a working knowledge of the Law and the Prophets.

So, Jesus apparently chose the apostles to show just whom he could use. That overwhelms me with encouragement. For his inner circle, Jesus chose a group that affirmed the trend we see from the Old Testament—only the weak and foolish need apply. (1 Corinthians 1:27)

Chapter 14

Apostolic Baggage

The apostles exhibited more *unapostolic* activity than *apostolic*. These were men of fear. Their fear overcame them as they fought against wind and wave, even when Jesus was asleep in their boat having told them, "Let us go to the other side." When Jesus says that, you will get there. Then, when Jesus, awakened from a refreshing wave-blessed sleep, stood and rebuked the waves, they were terrified. They never knew when to enjoy.

In spite of all that Jesus said about his resurrection, just prior to his crucifixion, they fearfully agreed to accompany him to Jerusalem knowing that *they* might die. Then after the crucifixion, they hid fearfully expecting to be captured and killed. To this cowering bunch, Jesus appeared in order to calm and encourage them.

Perhaps the most telling failure on their part revealed itself in their constant arguing over who among them was the greatest in the kingdom. Why might this have been so? First, these were street-level men drafted as executives into the greatest movement ever to happen in Israel. That is a heady place of power for a group of unsophisticated men. In politics, even sophisticates jockey to be photographed with men of power and influence. Should we expect anything less from these common workers?

Second, at mealtime in Israel at that time, people reclined around a low table in order of their rank. This means that every time they gathered to eat at a table, the question of *who sat where* presented itself. This made the argument a frequent affair by sheer tradition.

Third, the very graciousness of Jesus may have caused each one to think that Jesus considered him to be his favorite, thus providing fodder for the argument. Indeed, John informs us of his favored spot at the table by revealing that he was the one whom Jesus loved, who leaned against his breast. (John 21:20) That subtly informs us that he was next to Jesus at spot number one and simply means that, in order to speak to Jesus, John had to lean back against his chest.

Whatever the cause or causes, their arguing time apparently occupied more of their time than anything else they did. Not a good item for an apostolic resume.

Sons of Thunder

No one examples the tension among the apostles more than James and John. In Matthew 20:20-28, their power hunger moves them to hire their mother as a lobbyist to urge Jesus to give them the right-hand and left-hand positions. It was a private meeting that produced something vastly different from what they wanted (power hunger always does that), and initiated another apostolic fight.

Jesus responded to that fight with a leadership seminar that compared his kingdom to the kingdom of the pagan world (Gentiles). While they (the pagan world leaders) lord it over others and their great ones exercise authority over people, Jesus refuses that style for his kingdom. Instead, *"...whoever desires to become great among you, let him be your servant. And whoever desires to be first among you, let him be your slave...."* NKJ

Servanthood, oh so slowly, achieved some recognition in the apostles' minds. I understand. Nothing creates an agonizing rebellion in my flesh more than the call to servanthood. Servanthood flows from the heart of God, not from mine. Oh, how slowly I learn.

What grace Jesus exhibited in keeping the apostles on board and not replacing them. Indeed, Jesus chose *not many mighty.* God looks for the powerless, the losers, the inadequates, the weak and the foolish to accomplish his purposes. I am so glad!

Chapter 15

What? Me Understand?

The Gospels chronicle eloquently the apostles' lack of understanding. Obvious. It is hard to comprehend deep theologies when your mind is filled with self-serving arguments and resentments.

Perhaps the leading ongoing absence of discernment concerned Judas who escaped their radar as a potential traitor. Even at the table where Jesus established the event we call *communion* and washed the disciples' feet, when Judas arose to leave at Jesus' command to "Go do what you must do," the others thought he had gone to buy more food for the table or to give money to the poor. Amazing set of options in their minds. Jesus identified Judas as his betrayer when he opened the banquet by giving Judas the first bite from his own bowl. Incidentally, this act shows us that Judas sat at the *guest of honor* position at the table.

However, this was only one of the list of last-minute failures. When Jesus moved toward Peter to wash his feet (foot washing was the lowest job of the lowest slave partly because custom dictated that the bottom of the foot was the dirtiest part of the body), he attempted to halt the process. He obviously failed to see the redemptive act of Jesus at street level.

Then Peter, ever the *now* guy, asked why he couldn't follow Jesus *now,* having failed to hear the many predictions Jesus gave concerning his death at the hands of the religious leaders. He even boasted that he would be willing to die for him. He must have been shocked at Jesus' statement about his pending denial. Jesus, realizing the trauma approaching, assured them that their hearts should not be troubled.

In John 14, Jesus told the disciples that *"...the way you know,"* to which Thomas responded, *"we do not know where you are going, and how can we know the way?"* Remember that this conversation occurred at the end of three or four years of the finest teaching in all of eternity. They were *verrryy sloooow learnerrrrs.* Jesus must have fought discouragement as he stated, *"I am the way, the truth, and the life."* To reinforce this awesome declaration, he added, *"I am the way and the truth and the life. No one comes to the Father except through me. If you really knew me, you would know my Father as well. From now on, you do know him and have seen him."* (John 14:6-7)

Obviously, Jesus knew they still didn't know him. Their ignorance was quickly revealed: Philip said, *"Lord, show us the Father and that will be enough for us."* The frustration of Jesus rose to the surface as he responded, *"...how can you say, 'Show us the Father'?"*

If I were Jesus, I would have said, "Beam me up, Father. There is no intelligent life down here." His patient response was, *"Anyone who has seen me has seen the Father; ...."* (John 14)

I taught in a Christian college for six years and expected my students to know more than the apostles after just one year, much less four. So, let's go back and see how the apostles did earlier.

Off-Base Theology

In John 9, the disciples ask a very strange question: *"...who did sin, this man, or his parents, that he was born blind?"* This question ignores the obvious inability to sin before we are born; however, they borrowed this error from the Pharisees who believed that any sickness or disability was caused by a sin of the person. Though our actions do have consequences, even today we look for fault rather than ways we can help. Jesus stated clearly: *"Neither this man nor his parents sinned, but this happened so that the work of God might be displayed in his life. As long as it is day, we must do the work of him who sent me. Night is coming, when no one can work. While I am in the world, I am the light of the world."*

Constant Bickering

In Mark 9:33-34, Jesus asks: *"What were you arguing about on the road?"* But they kept quiet because on the way they had argued about who was the greatest. This arguing was so typical of the apostles that you find it occurring throughout the Gospels. Whether during mealtimes, walking times, resting times, teaching times, the question of who was greatest never left their minds or conversations.

Hostility Toward People

The apostles stopped people from doing good because they weren't part of their group, wanted to call fire down on a village because they were refused a night's lodging there, directed Jesus to send a hungry multitude away, and rebuked mothers for wanting Jesus to touch their children. When Jesus, along with Peter, James and John, descended from the Mount of Transfiguration, he found the rest of the apostles fighting with the people. How far can this list go? Perhaps John in recording the life of Jesus as beyond written capability, saves the apostles also from further recorded failures.

Clueless

Listen to these questions and statements to and about the apostles from Jesus and New Testament commentary: (NLT)

Don't you understand...? (repeatedly asked)

Won't you ever learn or understand?

If you can't understand this story, how will you understand all the others I am going to tell?

But they didn't understand a thing he said.

You don't have much faith.

Why are you so afraid? Do you still not have faith in me?

Not until the infusion of the Holy Spirit did understanding begin to congeal in their hearts and minds. That seems to be the only way our incompetences can be overcome for the glory of God.

Chapter 16

Bondage

At the end of Luke 9, three people gave a famous trio of conditions for following Jesus. Their offers exhibited how tenaciously the flesh clung to the ground among those who followed Jesus.

Emotion

The first disciple, overcome by his emotions, offers to follow Jesus *"...wherever you go."* Emotions, handy and dangerous at the same time, seldom follow rules of logic. One never says, "Based on the evidence I see, I shall now have this emotion." Emotions come. They are fickle. Emotions go. Often, I am willing to follow Jesus wherever I can take my favorite pillow or wherever I can muster my favorite food or wherever I don't *have* to eat certain food.

Jesus never seemed to try to elicit emotion. Indeed, in what we call "The Beatitudes," when Jesus said "Blessed are," the word "blessed" was a coin toss for the translator as to whether he would say "blessed" or "happy." The statements following his "Happy are" declarations are not often associated with happiness.

Knowing that this disciple's emotions needed a dose of reality, Jesus' response was, *"Foxes have holes and birds of the air have nests, but the Son of Man has nowhere to lay his head."*

Sleeping on the ground seldom produces great emotion. Some feel that *church* hasn't happened unless there is a great emotional charge or physical display. Others, bound by nostalgia, lack emotional fulfillment unless the stained glass or pews surround them. "It just doesn't *feel* like church," they would say. Serving and loving God reaches far deeper than our emotions and sustains us during times utterly devoid of emotion and comfort.

Money

Another disciple, invited by Jesus to follow him, begs a prior responsibility: *"Lord, let me first go and bury my father."* Now, what is wrong with this? It sounds like a good and loving family responsibility. Here is the catch: His father was not dead. They always buried people (still do in Middle East cultures) on the same day as their death. If the father was dead, this man wouldn't have been there to ask the question. What he was asking was to let him go home, and when his father was dead and he had received his inheritance, then he would come and follow Jesus. Security operated this man's heart more than loyalty.

I understand this concern. I confess that I have delayed responding to the commands of God in my life until I could see the security in advance. I confess this to my shame, because God always supplied in ways I failed to see in advance. Security rules now more than freedom in our country. We surround ourselves with

68

safety avoiding all risks, even the great risks of following our Lord.

Jesus quickly clarified this man's goals: *"Let the dead bury their own dead, but you go and preach the kingdom of God."* In other words, the spiritually dead seek such security. Let them bury the dead. Let them seek financial structure. There is no true security in this world. Rampant frauds and bankruptcies prove beyond debate that no company, no bank, no financial institution is beyond the reach of a good thief. So what security can we count on? *"Preach the kingdom of God."* Jesus puts it this way, *"But seek first the kingdom of God and his righteousness, and all these things shall be added to you."* Dangerous and unsafe, but wonderful and true. Just as the Levites had no inheritance with the tribes of Israel, because the Lord was their inheritance, so we walk in this world knowing it is not our home and our security is not with the local bank or the government, but with God.

Family Approval

Another disciple, who again proves that Jesus seems surrounded by the losers of this world, says, *"I will follow you, Lord; but first let me go back and say good-by to my family."* Once again, this sounds on the surface like a good family stance; however, what this man was saying was, "Let me go and get the approval of my family, then I will follow you." In that culture, they would not give you a *good bye* unless they approved of you and what you were doing. How many of us would even be in the kingdom were it based on a vote of our family? Many are disowned by their families when they choose to obey and follow Jesus.

To this person, Jesus responds most harshly: *"No one, having put his hand to the plow, and looking back, is fit for the kingdom of God."* On this earth, our natural families are so temporary. I am an Erwin. No one asked me if I wanted to be an Erwin. It just happened. Some in this temporary family I will not see beyond this earthly life. Some, thank God, have decided to join the *Family of Choice* that God offers us and will live forever. It pains me when I see people who love God allow unredeemed family to decide their spiritual futures.

Often we claim, "Blood is thicker than water." My answer is "Who's blood are you talking about?" If you go to Jesus for a theology of family, you are in trouble. He was harsh on our temporary families simply because in the most real sense, they often form bondages and spiritual jails. But even our natural or temporary families we love and treat more appropriately when we give our allegiance to God.

Amazing that Jesus would even choose to use the likes of us when we fill the contract to follow him with so many conditions.

Chapter 17

Peter, James and John, Inc.

Failed Fishermen

Documentaries usually catalog successes of great companies, rarely failures. That great documentary called The New Testament includes commentary on a famous fishing company that I call *Peter, James and John, Inc.*

Every report of their fishing exploits records a failure. Each record of their failure also notes that it occurred after fishing all night. One wonders if they did so much night fishing because they were embarrassed to be seen failing during daytime.

Being a church kid, throughout all my Sunday School days, I heard the names over and over, Peter, James and John. From all accounts shared with me, they constituted the inner circle, the ones Jesus felt closest to and wanted by his side, the ones most spiritually developed, the ones most likely to be corporate officials. They impressed me.

Now, though, after reading the Bible more thoroughly for myself, I see them in a different light. These men now seem to act more like the remedial class. Perhaps Jesus called them closest to himself because he couldn't trust them with the other guys. Perhaps they needed the close training the most.

Keep in mind that since they labored in regular jobs, they also failed the upward ladder of the religious (the only kind they had) school system as described earlier. Jesus obviously chose from the ordinary, even failed, crowd. Perhaps even the aggressiveness of Peter demanded a closeness to Jesus in order to keep him from destroying the rest of the apostles. Peter, likely oldest since he was the only one concerned about the temple tax, probably also felt the superiority of his age. In many ways, Peter represented lightening poised to strike even from a clear sky. Jesus needed him near.

Peter's aggressiveness found a match in James and John, brothers and *sons of thunder* as Jesus called them. Perhaps this was because of John's desire to obliterate a Samaritan village for lack of a vacant room. Perhaps Jesus reacted to the secret solicitation of the top administration and honor spots of James and John through their mother. So, in this famous corporation, we watch thunder and lightening constantly threatening. Jesus needed them close.

Peter, who rebuked Jesus for predicting his own death. Peter, who crashed and burned at the threat of his own death. Peter, who identified Jesus as the Messiah. Peter, who then finds himself rebuked as Satan. Peter, who chastened Jesus for stating, in the middle of a thronging crowd, that someone had touched him and virtue had gone out of him. Peter, who declares that he didn't touch Jesus. Peter, who was assuring Jesus that he needed no added virtue. Jesus needed Peter close.

Peter, who balked at permitting Jesus to wash his feet. Peter, who goes extreme in desiring a complete wash for himself. Peter, whose best military efforts to defend Jesus produced only the right ear of a servant. Peter, who failing in his highest affirmation, denies the one he loved. Peter needed to be close to Jesus.

John, who constantly exhibited the tension between himself and Peter. John, with small put-downs such as declaring himself a winner in a race with Peter to the empty tomb. John, who let us know he sat next to Jesus at the last supper. John, who let us know that Peter occupied the lowest seat at the table. John, who stopped someone from doing good because it threatened his exclusive franchise on Jesus. Jesus needed to keep John close.

Hopefully, you can see why I consider them, not the elite or most loved or most capable of the apostles, but the three who needed the most work, thus they stayed the closest. Whenever you hear someone telling you to "draw closer to Jesus," ignore the insult and rejoice that he uses the likes of us.

Chapter 18

After Graduation

If we consider John 13-17, commonly called the *upper room passages*, as graduation night message and ceremonies, we can then look to the future of the apostles to see what progress they made with their awesome learning. Have they moved from losers to winners, from jerks to giants? Well, yes…and no.

After this intense night of teaching, as Jesus entered what we call the *agony* and sweats blood, he asked his *remedial* class, Peter, James and John, to *watch* or pray for an hour. We know they entered this apostolic prayer by the sound of their snoring. When Jesus returned and awakened them, urging them again to pray for an hour, we observe them reentering their apostolic prayer and, again, we know by the sound of their snoring.

Surely they felt deeply disappointed in themselves. They knew they had let Jesus down, even though they didn't intend to do so. None-the-less, we have more evidence of their inadequacy. Perhaps, just perhaps, they considered, as we often do, just what they could do to atone for their failure. Sometimes when wives tearfully inform me that their husbands forgot their anniversary, I tell them, to their shock, that his forgetfulness is a good thing. Just gently remind him of his forgetfulness and in his guilt, your husband will give you a much better gift than he would have otherwise.

The Great Ear Slash

So, perhaps, Peter wonders how he can make it up to Jesus. His opportunity comes rapidly. Enter, soldiers. The temple guards arrive only to be met by Jesus offering himself to them, subsequently getting reorganized from falling all askew when they heard him say, *"I AM."* Peter seeing his chance, draws his sword and manages to get only the ear of Malchus, the chief priest's servant. I suppose you might want a man like Peter in your army, but at least he should improve his aim! Maybe you would not want him.

Of course, Peter's denial of Jesus along with his *following from afar* comes after graduation, also. Then after the crucifixion and resurrection, Jesus tells them to go to Galilee and wait for him. They go and wait, and wait, and wait. Finally, Peter decides that perhaps being an apostle demands greater patience than he can muster, so he returns to his old pursuits, pursuits he told Jesus at an earlier time were completely abandoned. Not only did he return, he talked seven of the apostles into going with him—fishing.

Though now Peter shows his true mettle, Jesus' only rebuke and instruction is *"If you love me, feed my sheep."* Then Peter shows his spirit further by seeming a bit perturbed that Jesus didn't have a stiff prophecy for John as he did for him.

But, we are not through. Peter decides that he is in charge of replacing Judas and orchestrates the choosing of Matthias, not by vote or discussion, but by casting lots or drawing straws as we would say. Will this dubious record ever end? No, but it does get interrupted.

Finally, Something Good

How the apostles managed to pull this one off we do not know. Obeying Jesus, they tarried (for 10 days) in Jerusalem waiting for the promised power from God. They achieved something they had never managed before—they achieved unity—they were in *one accord*. At that point, God filled them with the Holy Spirit, whom Jesus said would empower them and would speak of Jesus. Now, Peter stands *with the eleven*, a statement that could not have been made earlier.

Peter's thorough sermon indicates that the Holy Spirit had brought fruit to his life and clarified his mind. Prior to this point, we would have never guessed that Peter was so versed in the Scripture. The results brought 3,000 into the kingdom—people who were *pricked* in their hearts and wanted to know what to do. Before, Peter used his physical sword and only reaped an ear which Jesus had to repair. Now, he used the sword of the Lord and, with accurate aim toward the heart, reaps a great harvest.

Next we find another awesome result—it was Peter and John, the old antagonists now walking hand-in-hand, who made their way to the Temple and were used of God to heal the crippled man at the Gate Beautiful.

Further good—the power of God so flowed through Peter that people lined streets just so his shadow could fall on them and heal them. In truth, the Holy Spirit operated in the life of Peter. Then God offered Peter the greatest opportunity of all time—the hearts of the Gentile world. Peter, at first resistant to eating the unclean animals offered in a vision to him, finally obeys and goes to the house of Cornelius preaching the Gospel with great results. Now, the rest of the world was eligible to receive God's grace.

Peter now must defend his actions before the apostolic headquarters council. Why? Shouldn't the new believers and apostles rejoice in the work of grace for the world? They should, but they didn't. Finally the apostles accept and rejoice. The argument seemed over. No, we will revisit this controversy once again. No, twice.

Peter, now offered the Gentile world, …well, we would like to say begins the journey of redemption, but we cannot. Something happens that draws him back and off the stage. Maybe the fact that he had to defend himself before his brethren for preaching the Gospel to the *wrong* people took some wind out of his sails.

Finally, God turns to another vessel, equally unlikely, to reach the vast multitudes called Gentiles. No one opposed Jesus more vehemently than a guy named Saul of Tarsus. Saul, an educated, zealous, influential and hostile person makes his way toward Damascus to hunt down and kill Christians who are Jews. God intersects his life and Paul becomes an educated, zealous, influential and loving person whom God could use to send to the Gentiles.

Indeed, in God's sense of humor, no one would potentially hate Gentiles more than Saul, now Paul, along with hating Christians. Surprise! Paul so changed that we non-Jews owe a great debt to him. Paul's new theology closely reflected the nature and grace of Jesus. Later, when Peter, still locked in his traditions, fell prey to Judaizers (those who felt that the salvation of Jesus did not free them from the Law and traditions) and would not eat with Gentile believers, Paul openly rebuked him. There, in Peter's drift away from grace is our first revisit of apostolic incompetence. Our final visit of this argument still remains.

Whatever else we see, we must see that God never seems to use competence as a high point in his requirements. Perhaps not at all.

Chapter 19

Hardened Apostolic Hearts

Denominations are simply men taking *The Church*, the body of Christ, and reorganizing it according to human principles. Nowhere does this evidence itself more than in the apostles.

Several observations indicate that something terribly wrong had gone on in the very first expression of The Church. Denominational principles went to work. First, Jesus told them to go into all the world and preach the Gospel. Twenty years later, the apostles are still in Jerusalem—apparently establishing headquarters. Once they began to sense their power of administration and theological decision-making as apostles, they began to consolidate that power. This takes time, so the command to *go* needed to be postponed.

In the meantime, persecution had begun to force the believers out of Jerusalem and Israel and into other parts of the Gentile world where little thought would be given to the fact that they were Christians. However, so energized by the Holy Spirit was this band of believers, that everywhere they went, the Gospel was preached and more bands of believers were formed. So, in an odd way, the command to *go* was being obeyed, just not by the apostles.

In another odd way, we make a second observation. One reason the *go* command might have been delayed is because of another item that speaks denominationalism—at least *headquarterism*. An old philosophical statement rings with truth, *Power corrupts and absolute power tends to corrupt absolutely*. Once the attraction of the power of banded apostles lured them and they tasted of its authority, that taste graduated to bondage.

As a hangover from their *greatest in the kingdom* argument days, they knew that the power rested in the Jerusalem headquarters (just as they thought it rested in being near Jesus originally). And, if one of them obeyed Jesus and went out, he would lose his power of group authority and may never be consulted again. I wonder if any of the apostles spent sleepless nights struggling with the voice of Jesus versus the call of fleshly power. Jesus seemed to be losing at this point.

Taking a closer look, you must credit the early church with caring for its widows. This may be a first. No recorded material indicates that societal groups took care of widows prior to Jesus. The apostles were directly responsible for this activity and we honor them...but they failed. After enough complaints from Greek widows about being shorted in their distribution of food, Peter goes before the church and does a dismaying thing.

No, he did not admit failure. He should have. He should have simply said, "We have failed and we need you to help us make it right." Instead, he put what we today call *spin* on the situation and made statements that, though questionably conceived, could not easily be argued against. *"It would not be right for us to neglect the ministry of the word of God in order to wait on tables."* (Acts 6:2)

Aha! The humiliation during the feeding of the 5,000 comes home to meet Peter again. The apostles had such trouble reconciling passing out food and being the greatest in the kingdom. Anyway, after directing them to choose seven men full of the Spirit and wisdom, Peter seems to realize that the *word* was not enough, so he adds to the spin: *"...and [we] will give our attention to prayer and the ministry of the word."* (Acts 6:4)

Ah, who can argue against prayer and the word. The problem is that they *can* give their attention to prayer and the word and wait on tables at the same time. The catch is that they can't do that and be top headquarters people. It is beneath them. I know. I have been there. I know.

Three questions immediately come to mind. Will the apostles show fruit from this new emphasis on prayer and the word? Will we see clarity in their thinking and discernment? Will the newly chosen seven exhibit a decline in the prayer and the word now that they have to wait on tables? The answers are surprising.

More Baggage

Perhaps this move of Peter's carried the baggage of a much earlier event with Jesus.

> When evening came, the boat was in the middle of the lake, and he was alone on land. He saw the disciples straining at the oars, because the wind was against them. About the fourth watch of the night he went out to them, walking on the lake. He was about to pass by them, but when they saw him walking on the lake, they thought he was a ghost. They cried out, because they all saw him and were terrified.
>
> Immediately he spoke to them and said, "Take courage! It is I. Don't be afraid." Then he climbed into the boat with them, and the wind died down. They were completely amazed, for they had not understood about the loaves; their hearts were hardened.
>
> Mark 6:47-52

Now, what would harden an apostle's heart? Indeed, what would harden the hearts of the whole lot? Though the Scripture doesn't explain, the seriousness of the situation prompts a possibility. Remember that just before this incident, Jesus had fed a crowd of at least 5,000 people. He did this with only five loaves and two fish. What an awesome event that normally would seal the power of Jesus in their hearts and make them fearless. The opposite happened. Why?

Keep in mind that these men, whose prior lives were caught up in boring routine, served now as executives in the biggest happening ever seen in Israel. This is heady stuff, unusual power for such run-of-the-mill men. Understandable at this juncture why they fought over positions. Look at them standing with Jesus as he taught a very attentive crowd. See them receiving the admiring stares of the crowd.

Hear them apparently win an argument with Jesus about feeding the people. See them bring a ridiculously inadequate lunch to Jesus—five loaves (buns, we would call them) and two fish (we would probably call them bait). Now listen as Jesus gives them an executive job—have them sit down in groups of fifty and one hundred. This fit the view the apostles had of themselves. They were ordering people around and looking just like executives.

Then, things changed. Jesus blessed this diminutive meal, broke it, and broke it and broke it, and handed it to the apostles to distribute. Folks, Jesus turned the apostles into waiters. This must have grated on their executive minds. Perhaps they endured taunts from the crowd, "We thought you were executives! You are only waiters! You want a tip?" The hardening begins. Jesus had reduced their status in their minds and they began to entertain bitter thoughts. Just, perhaps!

Jesus isn't finished with them. After they fed the crowd and they were gorged with food from the Master's hands, Jesus turned the apostles into garbage collectors. Pick up what remains! Ouch! This is the ultimate insult, the ultimate embarrassment. The hearts were becoming like flint. The subject of their minds and perhaps conversations as they attempted to row across this endless lake in the face of a relentless wind might have been their disappointment in what Jesus expected them to do.

Take this bitter conclusion and throw it across time to the *reign* of the apostles. No more waiting on tables for those guys! They were in charge. Jesus might have wanted them to wait on tables, but that was for a past time, not for the present. Can you hear the echo...? "It is not good...to wait on tables...."

The *Deacon* Dilemma

What about these seven men? How did having to wait on tables affect their ministry? We are blessed to know. The next two chapters give us a glimpse at the ministry of two of the deacons and we discover they were more apostolic than the apostles. Is it possible to wait on tables and learn the word and pray? Anyone who, for the sake of sharing the Gospel, has labored at jobs in the secular world while serving a church knows the supporting grace of God and his miraculous intervention.

The Apostle Paul certainly seemed to be able to make tents and study and preach.

The *servant-hearted, others-centered* nature of Jesus escaped Peter but found a home in these deacons. The one thing Jesus struggled the most to achieve among his closest followers failed to bear fruit during this period of time. Obedience and fruit will come later, but not by vote of headquarters. Amazing that God would continue to use such inadequate people, isn't it? Ah, rejoice!

Chapter 20

So, They Studied and Prayed

When Peter announced the new organizational approach to the church in Acts 6, we must credit him for wanting to do a good thing—study the Word and pray. Apparently, he does so. In fact, during a prayer time for Peter on the roof of Simon the tanner's home in Joppa, God orchestrated a theological earthquake. In a vision Peter was told to eat every kind of unclean animal carried in a sheet let down from Heaven. Such a change demands repetition, which God provided. The earthquake bore fruit as a Gentile troop arrives to take him to Caesarea to the house of Cornelius.

Peter goes, preaches, observes the work of the Holy Spirit, then defends God's actions before the *council*. Peter continued his apostolic work that included being the chief spokesman for this new visitation of God. Although the Scripture records that all the apostles continued to preach the Gospel faithfully, seeds of human weeds had already been sowed in God's garden.

Perhaps the pain of having to defend the work of God before the church which also lived under the order to preach this good news to *every creature* caused Peter to carefully consider any action that might bring him before such a council again. Perhaps that is why he hesitated to walk through the open door offered to the Gentiles. Perhaps his outspoken but eventually effective approach created a division that frequently exists even to this day.

Evangelism Versus Administration

Peter was the evangelist. John might be labeled evangelist, also. The other apostles seemed to be the organizers and decision makers. I have observed many churches grow hostile toward a pastor whom they consider to be only an evangelist and not a pastor/teacher. They encourage him to *move on* even offering the *left foot* of fellowship. Just as frequently, these men, zealous for souls, may overstep some arbitrary boundary of the organization and line up for their appearance before the *council*. However, the evangelist seems never to be a member of the council. For one thing, you need someone who is *there* in order to have meetings. Evangelists are usually elsewhere.

All this I say in order to bring a most interesting event to your attention. Another council meeting occurred because of the disturbing grace and salvation of God. Here is the cause.

Paul, most likely to succeed as an ambitious Pharisee, is now God's new one-man speeding tank against Satan. He and his sidekick, Barnabas (the encourager) enjoyed the greatest of success among the Gentiles. Rapidly happening, if you spoke of *The Church*, you spoke of the *Gentiles*. Unfortunately, this rattled some cages in Jerusalem. The large number of Pharisee Jews who populated the Jerusalem church had also corrupted its theology. They complained that these Gentiles lacked circumcision and should not be accepted. They even sent what we call *Judaizers* to the places of Paul's success to argue that now the new believers needed circumcision. Paul and Barnabas argued strongly against them.

Now, we must ask some questions. Where are the praying and studying apostles? Where is the understanding of God's grace? Where is the teaching that should have corrected this mistake? Where is the decision made after Peter's mission to Cornelius? Missing, missing, missing. So, what does this council do? They call Paul and Barnabas back to Jerusalem for their *called-on-the-carpet* time.

This action typifies headquarters mentality. In danger of losing *control* over the actions of God, they cave in to the demands of those noisiest and closest to them—the Judaizers. Perhaps being an *apostle* could subject one to a vote or recall in the future. Surely John would be telling them over and over, *"The law came by Moses; grace and truth by Jesus Christ."* Whatever happened, it is now Paul and Barnabas giving account for their actions, not the Judaizers.

When the council met and began their lively debate, Peter finally arose and addressed the group, forced to argue, once again, in behalf of the good news to the

Gentiles. Indeed, Peter introduced the first show of humility (something headquarters has only heard about) by reminding them that:

> "He made no distinction between us and them, for he purified their hearts by faith. Now then, why do you try to test God by putting on the necks of the disciples a yoke that neither we nor our fathers have been able to bear? No! We believe it is through the grace of our Lord Jesus that we are saved, just as they are."
> Acts 15:9-11

The lively debate ceases as they listen carefully to what Paul and Barnabas report of God's goodness and action. Finally, the council remembers the prophecies of Scripture (funny how their study missed this earlier) and declare:

> After this I will return
> and rebuild David's fallen tent.
> Its ruins I will rebuild,
> and I will restore it,
> that the remnant of men
> may seek the Lord,
> and all the Gentiles
> who bear my name,
> says the Lord, who does these things
> that have been known for ages.
> Acts 15:16-18

But look who does the talking—James! Look who makes the decision—James! Look who then shows how little he understands—James! If there was a first Pope, it wasn't Peter, it was James! Peter, forced to defend his own vision and encounters with Gentiles again, drops down the scale of authority. Perhaps Peter spent too much time evangelizing to solidify his position at headquarters.

Proclamation

So James crafts a letter releasing the Gentiles from the need to be circumcised. However, in typical headquarters fashion, certain requirements are to be met. What are they? We see them in Acts 15:19-21.

Abstain from food sacrificed to idols.

Abstain from blood.

Abstain from the meat of strangled animals.

Abstain from sexual immorality.

What!!? Abstaining from sexual immorality was fine, but the other three are hangovers from the law that crashed in Peter's vision. Perhaps these men prayed and studied less than they publicly indicated. Those who work in any headquarters know that frequent pronouncements demand unnecessary and arbitrary actions of employees. Why? Control and power and position rule hearts more than Scripture and love.

Wait a minute! Didn't Jesus say he would build his church? Yes! And he was building the church all over the known world; however, headquarters now had little or nothing to do with the building. In fact, if Jesus were not building his church, it would have faded off the face of the earth long ago. But why would he use these men who seem to get the instructions so wrong or apply them so unjustly? Further proof that God uses jerks. That is all he has available. However, there is no shortage of us jerks.

This story does not end with this letter. Headquarters sent two men with Paul and Barnabas to make sure this letter is read accurately to the people and so they can confirm by mouth. Just like headquarters. After reading the letter and encouraging the people, these men return home, satisfied that all is now well.

The Gentiles receive the letter joyfully. They probably had no plans to drink blood or eat meat from strangled animals or commit sexual immorality, but the meat offered to idols was the only kind of meat available to them in the markets. Paul had to clarify that requirement later by telling them this meant not to eat meat that a host specifically states is pledged to an idol. But, at least they didn't have to be circumcised! Rejoice!

Well, that segment is over. We know that the apostles were definitely among the *weak and foolish* whom God chooses to use. We can admire them as heroes, but they weren't heroic. They were as much in need of the grace of God as we are. Whatever good happened from their lives issued not from their deep thinking but straight from the work of the Holy Spirit overcoming their incompetence.

With great humility and joy, we can hear the words of the Holy Spirit through Paul in 2 Corinthians 4:1-3:

> Therefore, since through God's mercy we have this ministry, we do not lose heart. Rather, we have renounced secret and shameful ways; we do not use deception, nor do we distort the word of God. On the contrary, by setting forth the truth plainly we commend ourselves to every man's conscience in the sight of God.

God has not given me (or you) this ministry because we are more eloquent, good looking, influential or wealthy than others. No, those attributes work against us. God has given us ministry simply out of his mercy. If only one person ever shows up to hear me, that is one person more than I deserve. But, Oh, his Mercy!

Chapter 21

Paul, the Great and the Gory

Paul, from whom we receive much understanding of church practice, organization and theology, now continues his ministry along with Barnabas. However, something new drops into Paul's heart—a nervousness, an anxiety, a harshness reminiscent of his Pharisaical days. Maybe the debate at the council got to him in ways we have not considered.

What might run through Paul's mind as he observes men, of lesser intellect and training, attempting to lead a new movement yet not having a firm grasp on the grace and nature of Jesus? Do you suppose that he, once eligible to be Chief Priest in Israel, thought of how much better job he could do? Do you suppose some old ambitions brushed the edges of his heart? He could arguably have been the most effective apostle in the room. Do you suppose he had that thought? We do not know, but something dealt him a blow.

Paul gives us his perspective on that eventful meeting in Jerusalem in Galatians 2:

> Then fourteen years later I went back to Jerusalem again, this time with Barnabas; and

Titus came along, too. I went there because God revealed to me that I should go. While I was there I talked privately with the leaders of the church. I wanted them to understand what I had been preaching to the Gentiles. I wanted to make sure they did not disagree, or my ministry would have been useless. And they did agree. They did not even demand that my companion Titus be circumcised, though he was a Gentile.

Even that question wouldn't have come up except for some so-called Christians there—false ones, really—who came to spy on us and see our freedom in Christ Jesus. They wanted to force us, like slaves, to follow their Jewish regulations. But we refused to listen to them for a single moment. We wanted to preserve the truth of the Good News for you.

And the leaders of the church who were there had nothing to add to what I was preaching. (By the way, their reputation as great leaders made no difference to me, for God has no favorites.) They saw that God had given me the responsibility of preaching the Good News to the Gentiles, just as he had given Peter the responsibility of preaching to the Jews. For the same God who worked through Peter for the benefit of the Jews worked through me for the benefit of the Gentiles. In fact, James, Peter, and John, who were known as pillars of the church, recognized the gift God had given me, and they accepted Barnabas and me as their co-workers. They encouraged us to keep preaching to the Gentiles, while they continued their work with the Jews. The only thing they suggested was that we remember to help the poor, and I have certainly been eager to do that. NLT

Paul tells us that this group of leaders added nothing to his ministry except to recognize and approve it, but the intensity of the battle affected him. How? Let us consider.

Dissent

First, Paul refuses to take Mark along on their journey. Mark had apparently faltered in a previous journey and Paul, in spite of the pleas of Barnabas, was unwilling to issue grace. The debate becomes so adamant that Barnabas and Paul split and go their separate ways. We know that later Paul would relent and ask for Mark to come along, but something is growling in his heart at this moment as we can see in the next event. The growl breaks into a bark and then bites in Acts 16.

Welcome Timothy!

Watch Out for the Cobras!

In the town of Lystra, Paul met an outstanding young believer named Timothy. Everyone spoke well of him and Paul invited him to join his missionary journey. Timothy agreed. One catch—Timothy's Gentile father! Here is how Acts 16:3 describes the outcome:

> Paul wanted to have him go on with him. And he took him and circumcised him because of the Jews who were in that region, for they all knew that his father was Greek. NLT

Paul! Paul! What has happened in your mind? After such powerful defense of your ministry to the Gentiles, now you take one and circumcise him because of expected ministry to the Jews. Yet that ministry never happened. Instead, God sent Paul to Macedonia in response to a vision. Paul, did you ever apologize to Timothy? Did you ever feel any remorse?

Later, Paul urges Timothy to stir up the gift that is in him and reminds him that God has not given us a spirit of timidity and fear. Is it possible that Timothy wasn't timid at all? Is it possible that Timothy might have been afraid of what Paul might require of him next time? We don't know.

What we can see is that Paul, great as he was, found a place or two to show that he actually fit in with the rest of us jerks God has called. In fact, after describing himself as the least of the apostles (which is still not a bad position), he moves to describing himself as the least of the saints (still nothing to feel badly about), then declares his reality as the chiefest of sinners. Now he has come face to face with the rest of us.

Only Paul achieved the qualifications to say *knowledge puffs up, love builds up*. Had any other apostle said it, people would consider it bitter grapes. Paul fully understood that wealth of knowledge merely adds to our pride.

Pride happens to be the worst of sins. Pride split Heaven and formed Hell. Now we better understand why God chooses the weak and foolish. Paul speaks legitimately. Welcome to jerkhood. The prerequisite to sainthood.

Chapter 22

The Opening Parenthesis

John's preaching moved people. Something other than rote lecturing lined the roads with people from Jerusalem and the surrounding area to hear, repent and be baptized. Was it his style? Partly, perhaps. He dressed outside the box in camel's hair shirts. Perhaps such shirts lacked comfort and generated fiery sermons. At least, he avoided generating a "John the Baptist hair-shirt" sales booth. His choice of food, locusts and wild honey, prevented invitations to many business or social lunches. Living in the wilderness made it difficult to get in touch with him, anyway. Simply catching the locusts and rescuing the honey in the wilderness created a "different" style of living.

So, why did so many come to listen? Was it his message? Surely it was. Why did they ask him if he was the Messiah? He must have been an outstanding orator whose simple lifestyle added to his credibility and whose message, *Repent, for the kingdom of heaven is at hand*, captured hearts as none before him had done. Simply put, folks—He was good! The best!

Being so popular failed to corrupt him as he spoke with great directness and honesty to both soldier and king. The latter got him in serious trouble. Many might long to do what he did—identify and baptize the

Messiah—but few would seek his style or wish his consequences.

After he baptized Jesus, his prior criticism of Herod finally resulted in his being arrested. Already, John could see his own area of influence weaken as many of his own disciples left to follow Jesus. John, with unusual insight, happily accepted diminished ministry and recognized Jesus as the bridegroom empowered with unlimited supplies of the Holy Spirit.

New Lifestyle

However, John fell into a web he surely could not foresee. Being arrested surely meant the end of everything, unless, of course, this new deliverer/messiah fulfilled expectations and rescued him while throwing off the shackles of Rome. The wilderness didn't prepare John for the palace. Herod's wife despised John, but Herod enjoyed him. Herod feared John, yes, but he also enjoyed him. Maybe such eloquence rarely reached the palace. Wait!! If Herod liked John, why arrest him? Ah, the constantly lurking fury, Mrs. Herod, nursed the ultimate grudge. "Who is this grizzly upstart who thinks he can criticize our marriage? I have ways to handle him."

In the face of this fury, Herod had no choice but to take the popular preacher into protective custody.

Perhaps she occasionally sneered at Herod for harboring such a dangerous, deadly, righteousness requiring person (I'm sure more words were used to disdain him) hardly befitting the king. At any rate, Herod wanted John around regardless of his wife's fury. He often listened to him, though he never understood him. But such good preaching was worth the puzzlement. I can almost hear the conversation.

"Hey preacher-boy, preach me a sermon!"

"Okay, what subject do you want?"

"Well, I like that kingdom thing you do. Kinda' scary, but you sure do it well."

Well, preaching to the king is rather heady. Many would give up everything for such an opportunity. If his disciples were leaving him for Jesus, at least the king saw his worth. Further, the clothing of the palace, the food of the palace, the beds of the palace far exceeded anything he had ever experienced before. Rather relaxing after such prior sacrifices.

Palace Chaplain

Now, it becomes obvious what had happened—John had become the palace chaplain. In the presence of such ease, one's focus changes. One must be careful not to insult the king. Politics, you know. Perhaps we can make changes from within the system. Palace chaplain does have its influence, you know. But keep in mind that

Herod's befuddlement shows that truth always befuddles the powerful, even watered-down truth.

As palace chaplain, John enjoyed certain freedoms. He certainly had the ear of Herod. That would be all the protection he needed, surely. His disciples had access to him. What more could he add to all the comforts he now enjoyed? Maybe, as he conversed with Herod and basked in all that power, then discussed with his disciples what expectations of the Messiah that didn't seem to be fulfilled, the moment of doubt overtook him. So, this prophet of the kingdom sent two of his own disciples to Jesus to ask him if he actually was the Messiah or should we look for another.

Palaces and prophets and messiahs mix very poorly. Two of them have to surrender and palaces don't surrender. John waits to hear and the only message brought back to him kicks his heart back to reality. If I may paraphrase, "Tell John that the Spirit is still here." You see, when John began his ministry, the only clue given to him by the Father as to the identity of the Messiah would be seeing the Spirit coming down and remaining. He had seen and now he sees or hears again.

I wonder if he realized what had happened to him. Was he now at rest? Did he convert, at least in his mind, back to the locust, wild honey, hair shirt and leather girdle mentality? I like to think that he did. In my carnal thinking, this would be the ideal time for God to arrange his release, but politicians and scorned wives don't listen to God.

Disaster Party

The convention of the Herod Party included a little of what might be called in our modern day, "adult entertainment." Herod's stepdaughter certainly knew how to do it. In fact, her effective erotic dance so pleased the conventioneers that Herod knew he had found a vote-getter, so he, reeling from his own lust, offered whatever this "girl with the moves" wanted, up to half the kingdom. But this showgirl only understood the erotic. She needed counsel from her mother. She, the queen, certainly would have scoped this out ahead of time.

"Go back and tell him you want the head of John on a platter. Tell him you want it right now!" Mrs Herod knew better than to give him opportunity to ponder or to do this "repenting" he had heard so much about lately. Right now!

The terrified Herod, unable to overcome the political promise or gauge the ethics of campaign contributions, caved in and demonstrated that being liked by the king won't save your head. Being the palace chaplain doesn't mean that the palace sees you as anything other than entertainment or, perhaps, to use you as feigned evidence that the palace is interested in spiritual things.

That head on a platter must have brought screams of disgust from the dancing girl as she delivered it and heard the "Ahh" of a satisfied mother. Herod, trembling, cradled his head in his hands. It was over.

So intensely this ghastly moment hung on him. When he heard of the ministry of Jesus, he thought, maybe hoped, that this was John come back to life. Herod believed in the resurrection. He sent for Jesus. Perhaps Jesus would become the new palace chaplain. Jesus rejected the opportunity. Ha! That will cost him his head.

But the Messiah lived, and nothing Herod could do would stop him. Kill him if you wish, but watch a power you can't imagine raise him to life forever. Never underestimate the resurection.

As for John, though he demonstrated his weakness and doubt from that castle, thus establishing his place among the weak and foolish, Jesus elevated him immensely (as he does all of us) with these dramatic words: *"I tell you, among those born of women there is no one greater than John; yet the one who is least in the kingdom of God is greater than he."* (Luke 7:28)

PART THREE

A Heart for the Flawed

The Spirit of the LORD is upon me,
Because he has anointed me
To preach the gospel to the poor;
He has sent me to heal the
brokenhearted,
To proclaim liberty to the captives
And recovery of sight to the blind,
To set at liberty those who are
oppressed;
To proclaim the acceptable year of the
LORD.
Luke 4:18–19 NKJ

I hate pride and arrogance,
evil behavior and perverse speech.
Proverbs 8:13

Chapter 23

Weak and Foolish? There Are So Many of Them!

Why would God choose to work with the weak and foolish? To me, the answer is simple: God loves people. If you look at the people of the world, very few reach the winner's circle or the president's desk or the castle of the wealthy or the star of the silver screen. True, the world sees life through the eyes of the elite and longs to copy them. Not so our Lord. He sees life through the eyes of the needy and low. Does God oppose the elite? No, only the proud. But show me the elite who are not proud.

Then, how can we fit Paul himself into this *not many mighty* category when the fact is, he was a man of influence and reputation? The answer is simple. Paul, like Jesus, made himself of no reputation. From this position, he could speak to anyone and especially to the situation of his past. Our theme verses come from his pen as prompted by the Holy Spirit.

> Brothers, think of what you were when you were called. Not many of you were wise by human standards; not many were influential; not many were of noble birth. But God chose the foolish things of the world to shame the wise; God chose the weak things

of the world to shame the strong. He chose the lowly things of this world and the despised things–and the things that are not–to nullify the things that are, so that no one may boast before him.

It is because of him that you are in Christ Jesus, who has become for us wisdom from God–that is, our righteousness, holiness and redemption. Therefore, as it is written: "Let him who boasts boast in the Lord."
1 Corinthians 1:26–31

The reduction of Paul brings an interesting set of thoughts. We know that he had bad eyesight. We know that his voice was weak, perhaps irritating. Legend indicates that he was short and humpbacked. Can you see him saying to people, "I am your apostle."? Indeed, there were those who called themselves apostles who looked like an apostle is supposed to look. Perhaps they were tall, handsome, strong bass voice, hair swept back and ready for television. At any rate, Paul would have described them as a mile wide but only an inch deep. He hated having to defend his apostolic position. Only the anointing and power of God made up his resume.

One great queen of England described the *not many mighty* passage as rescuing her for the Kingdom. She remarked, "It does not say 'not *any* mighty,' so the Gospel is for me, also."

Thorn

So powerful looms the corruption of success and fame, that God, out of kindness we won't understand this side of heaven, had to cripple Paul in some way after an exceedingly great vision given to him. Here is how Paul describes:

> To keep me from becoming conceited because of these surpassingly great revelations, there was given me a thorn in my flesh, a messenger of Satan, to torment me. Three times I pleaded with the Lord to take it away from me. But he said to me, "My grace is sufficient for you, for my power is made perfect in weakness." Therefore I will boast all the more gladly about my weaknesses, so that Christ's power may rest on me. That is why, for Christ's sake, I delight in weaknesses, in insults, in hardships, in persecutions, in difficulties. For when I am weak, then I am strong.
>
> 2 Corinthians 12:7-10

In order for this *thorn* to keep him from being conceited, it, in my mind, had to be something embarrassing, even humiliating. Otherwise, he could have managed the conceit. Perhaps his eyes ran with matter that looked like a terrible cold and caused people to turn away repulsed. Whatever the thorn was, it would cause people to say, "He has no reason to be conceited."

Head Count

If anyone possessed the power and mind to speak eloquently and think deeply, Paul did. When he met on Mars Hill in Athens with the thinkers of his day, his reasoning matched their best. One problem: He left few, if any, believers and built no great church there. Athens is remarkably absent from the list of the churches of Asia in Revelations.

Perhaps this was a watershed moment for Paul. After seeing how little his best shot accomplished, he returned to the one thing that he knew had God's stamp of approval. He describes this way:

> When I came to you, brothers, I did not come with eloquence or superior wisdom as I proclaimed to you the testimony about God. For I resolved to know nothing while I was with you except Jesus Christ and him crucified. I came to you in weakness and fear, and with much trembling. My message and my preaching were not with wise and persuasive words, but with a demonstration of the Spirit's power, so that your faith might not rest on men's wisdom, but on God's power.
>
> 1 Corinthians 2:1-5

Amazing that Paul would be the one to say, "I resolved to know nothing...." However, success in the world of man does not translate into the kingdom of

God. However, we elevate the wealthy or the beautiful or the famous if they espouse Christianity, often to our embarrassment. Indeed God describes his success story through the pen of Paul in this way:

> Therefore, as God's chosen people, holy and dearly loved, clothe yourselves with compassion, kindness, humility, gentleness and patience. Bear with each other and forgive whatever grievances you may have against one another. Forgive as the Lord forgave you. And over all these virtues put on love, which binds them all together in perfect unity.
>
> Let the peace of Christ rule in your hearts, since as members of one body you were called to peace. And be thankful. Let the word of Christ dwell in you richly as you teach and admonish one another with all wisdom, and as you sing psalms, hymns and spiritual songs with gratitude in your hearts to God. And whatever you do, whether in word or deed, do it all in the name of the Lord Jesus, giving thanks to God the Father through him.
>
> Colossians 3:12-17

Paul's experience with the religious world, the secular world and his own walk with God must have fueled his wisdom in a letter to Timothy:

But godliness with contentment is great gain. For we brought nothing into the world, and we can take nothing out of it. But if we have food and clothing, we will be content with that. People who want to get rich fall into temptation and a trap and into many foolish and harmful desires that plunge men into ruin and destruction. For the love of money is a root of all kinds of evil. Some people, eager for money, have wandered from the faith and pierced themselves with many griefs.

But you, man of God, flee from all this, and pursue righteousness, godliness, faith, love, endurance and gentleness.

1 Timothy 6:6-11

Worth the Price

However, to my way of thinking, Paul reaches his highest moment of expression, his greatest wisdom, his glorious success as the Holy Spirit moves him to clarify for all time the achievement of salvation. We read the proclamation and rejoice:

For it is by grace you have been saved, through faith—and this not from yourselves, it is the gift of God—not by works, so that no one can boast. For we are God's workmanship, created in Christ Jesus to do good works, which God prepared in advance for us to do.

Ephesians 2:8-10

Paul now knew that salvation belongs to the masses, the regular, the unknown, the hoi polloi, the bumpkins, the trash, the incompetent, the weak, the foolish...me!

Chapter 24

The Power Flow

Throughout the kingdoms of the world, whether democracies or dictatorships, leaders vacuum power from those at the bottom and collect it at the top. Leaders gather followers and their money in order to empower themselves. The three main articles of *faith* of all politicians are:

1. Get in power.

2. Stay in power.

3. Increase your power.

But what about the system God sets up in the example of Jesus and in our hearts? First, our power comes from God himself, not from some earthly source. John the Baptist describes Jesus this way in Matthew 3:11:

> "I baptize you with water for repentance. But after me will come one who is more powerful than I, whose sandals I am not fit to carry. He will baptize you with the Holy Spirit and with fire."

Jesus, fulfilling this prophecy, completes the heavenly power flow by saying to his apostles in Acts 1:8:

"But you will receive power when the Holy Spirit comes on you; and you will be my witnesses in Jerusalem, and in all Judea and Samaria, and to the ends of the earth."

Never, in all of this prophecy, do we see Jesus requiring a list of competency. These are all power flows to the incompetent. Why? Because that is who he uses.

Jesus himself made his power flow clear in the clientele of his anointing. Just in case we miss these implications, he even connects rewards to the direction of the power flow. The following two passages from Matthew make it very clear that the weak should be the focus of our ministry. He boils it down even to the thirsty, the hungry, the stranger, the naked, the sick and the prisoner. And just in case we rationalize ourselves out of the coverage, Jesus uses a generalization that we dare not miss—if we ignore the least of these, we have ignored Jesus.

"He who receives you receives me, and he who receives me receives the one who sent me. Anyone who receives a prophet because he is a prophet will receive a prophet's reward, and anyone who receives a righteous man because he is a righteous man will receive a righteous man's reward. And if anyone gives even a cup of cold water to one of these little ones because he is my disciple, I tell you the truth, he will certainly not lose his reward." Matthew 10:40–42

"Then the King will say to those on his right, 'Come, you who are blessed by my Father; take your inheritance, the kingdom prepared for you since the creation of the world. For I was hungry and you gave me something to eat, I was thirsty and you gave me something to drink, I was a stranger and you invited me in, I needed clothes and you clothed me, I was sick and you looked after me, I was in prison and you came to visit me.'

"Then the righteous will answer him, 'Lord, when did we see you hungry and feed you, or thirsty and give you something to drink? When did we see you a stranger and invite you in, or needing clothes and clothe you? When did we see you sick or in prison and go to visit you?'

"The King will reply, 'I tell you the truth, whatever you did for one of the least of these brothers of mine, you did for me.'

"Then he will say to those on his left, 'Depart from me, you who are cursed, into the eternal fire prepared for the devil and his angels. For I was hungry and you gave me nothing to eat, I was thirsty and you gave me nothing to drink, I was a stranger and you did not invite me in, I needed clothes and you did not clothe me, I was sick and in prison and you did not look after me.'

"They also will answer, 'Lord, when did we see you hungry or thirsty or a stranger or needing clothes or sick or in prison, and did not help you?'

"He will reply, 'I tell you the truth, whatever you did not do for one of the least of these, you did not do for me.'

"Then they will go away to eternal punishment, but the righteous to eternal life."
Matthew 25:34–46

Perhaps the greatest example of all such power flows occurs in John 13. In the first three verses, we discover three aspects of Jesus that find fulfillment in one act:

First, he was going to show the full extent of his love.

Second, he knew who he was.

Third, he had all power.

The love of God is always an agape love, a totally unconditional and others-centered love. That alone examples complete one-way power flow. Now, the question is how he is going to show that *full extent* of his love. Please note that this is before the crucifixion.

Next, what does one do when he knows who he is. For one thing, if you know who you are, you never have to prove anything to anyone. You are impervious to the taunts and insults of men. You know the truth. When you know who you are, no job is beneath you or above you.

Finally, if you have all power, you are in danger of complete corruption. Here is Jesus with absolute power. How is he going to show his love and use his power without corruption? Let us see the answer in Scripture:

> It was just before the Passover Feast. Jesus knew that the time had come for him to leave this world and go to the Father. Having loved his own who were in the world, he now showed them the full extent of his love.
>
> The evening meal was being served, and the devil had already prompted Judas Iscariot, son of Simon, to betray Jesus. Jesus knew that the Father had put all things under his power, and that he had come from God and was returning to God; so he got up from the meal, took off his outer clothing, and wrapped a towel around his waist. After that, he poured water into a basin and began to wash his disciples' feet, drying them with the towel that was wrapped around him.
>
> He came to Simon Peter, who said to him, "Lord, are you going to wash my feet?"
>
> Jesus replied, "You do not realize now what I am doing, but later you will understand."
>
> "No," said Peter, "you shall never wash my feet."

Jesus answered, "Unless I wash you, you have no part with me."

"Then, Lord," Simon Peter replied, "not just my feet but my hands and my head as well!"

Jesus answered, "A person who has had a bath needs only to wash his feet; his whole body is clean. And you are clean, though not every one of you." For he knew who was going to betray him, and that was why he said not every one was clean.

When he had finished washing their feet, he put on his clothes and returned to his place. "Do you understand what I have done for you?" he asked them. "You call me 'Teacher' and 'Lord,' and rightly so, for that is what I am. Now that I, your Lord and Teacher, have washed your feet, you also should wash one another's feet. I have set you an example that you should do as I have done for you. I tell you the truth, no servant is greater than his master, nor is a messenger greater than the one who sent him. Now that you know these things, you will be blessed if you do them.
John 13:1–17

The answer to our question is simple—Jesus washed their feet. That happened to be the lowest slave job available. If a man owned any servants, the lowest ranked servant would wash the feet of guests. If a man was too poor to have servants, the host himself would wash feet but it was an admission of his low estate. Jesus could do this job only if he knew who he was. Also, remember that the bottom of the feet was considered to be the dirtiest part of the body in that day. Amazing that his love and power brought him to the dirtiest part of our bodies. Take note.

He Commands

In this servant act, this totally others-centered act, he also showed how he loved people and then later commands us to love one another as he has loved us. Indeed, he appointed that servant-hearted love as the means by which the world would know we belonged to him.

Here, we see the only way we can use power without being corrupted. If our power does not flow to the benefit of the weak, the dirty, etc., we are corrupt. Such simplicity!

Jesus never sought to avoid the criticisms of his enemies. He never asked, "What will people think?" When criticism flowed, he responded with simple illustrations. For instance:

> Tax collectors and other notorious sinners often came to listen to Jesus teach. This made the Pharisees and teachers of religious law complain that he was associating

with such despicable people—even eating with them! So Jesus used this illustration: "If you had one hundred sheep, and one of them strayed away and was lost in the wilderness, wouldn't you leave the ninety–nine others to go and search for the lost one until you found it? And then you would joyfully carry it home on your shoulders. When you arrived, you would call together your friends and neighbors to rejoice with you because your lost sheep was found. In the same way, heaven will be happier over one lost sinner who returns to God than over ninety–nine others who are righteous and haven't strayed away!

Luke 15:1-7 NLT

Indeed, against his self-righteous and aloof critics, Jesus leveled a direct and earth-shaking prophecy:

"I tell you the truth, the tax collectors and the prostitutes are entering the kingdom of God ahead of you. For John came to you to show you the way of righteousness, and you did not believe him, but the tax collectors and the prostitutes did. And even after you saw this, you did not repent and believe him."

Matthew 21:31–32

Jesus makes life simple. "I am your example. Do as I have done. Then you will be blessed." What else do I need to know? Once I feel that I have risen above the position of *jerk*, I must never forget to grab the hands of those around me and pull them up.

Chapter 25

The Anointing

So much evidence abounds on the inclination of God's heart and the direction of his attention that we must follow that trail. The words *Messiah* and *Christ* are identical, the first Hebrew, the second Greek, so they both mean *anointed* or more specifically *the anointed one.*

Because of the expectations of the Messiah, the meaning gradually drifted to an additional meaning, the Deliverer. Consequently, when Jesus announced, after a reading of Isaiah 61, that he was the fulfillment of the prophecy, thus the Messiah, all the expectations rushed to the forefront of the listeners' minds along with the disbelief that Jesus could be the one. More than anything, they wanted deliverance from Rome. More than anything, as evidenced by the expectations of the apostles, they wanted to be set up, after deliverance, as the rulers of the world. Jesus did not meet those expectations.

Indeed, in my experience, I have noticed that when any teacher/preacher expressed that he "felt the anointing," the results were merely louder speech, increased physical activity, and, more likely than not, legalistic aggressiveness. To my sorrow, I never in all my early years heard anyone describe the activity that the anointing produced in Jesus as *anointing.*

However, if we are faithful to Scripture, we must examine what that anointing activity that motivated Jesus might or should produce in us. Let us see what the Scripture says:

> The Spirit of the Sovereign LORD is on me, because the LORD has anointed me to preach good news to the poor. He has sent me to bind up the brokenhearted, to proclaim freedom for the captives and release from darkness for the prisoners, to proclaim the year of the LORD's favor and the day of vengeance of our God, to comfort all who mourn, and provide for those who grieve in Zion—to bestow on them a crown of beauty instead of ashes, the oil of gladness instead of mourning, and a garment of praise instead of a spirit of despair. They will be called oaks of righteousness, a planting of the LORD for the display of his splendor.
>
> They will rebuild the ancient ruins and restore the places long devastated; they will renew the ruined cities that have been devastated for generations. Aliens will shepherd your flocks; foreigners will work your fields and vineyards. And you will be called priests of the LORD, you will be named ministers of our God. You will feed on the wealth of nations, and in their riches you will boast.
>
> Instead of their shame my people will receive a double portion, and instead of

disgrace they will rejoice in their inheritance; and so they will inherit a double portion in their land, and everlasting joy will be theirs.

"For I, the LORD, love justice; I hate robbery and iniquity. In my faithfulness I will reward them and make an everlasting covenant with them."
Isaiah 61:1–8

How can we miss the direction of the power and interest of the anointing? Just note the beneficiaries:

The poor.

The brokenhearted.

The captives.

Prisoners in darkness.

Those out of favor.

Those who need God to provide vengeance.

The mourners.

Those in despair.

Ruined and devastated places.

Those in shame and disgrace.

Those who have suffered injustice.

Those who have been robbed.

Those who have suffered the effects of iniquity.

The typical response to these types of people expresses itself in blame: "If they can't live right, they deserve what they get." And that statement is probably true. The problem is that God seems more interested in redemption than blame. If ever my heart wraps itself around the value of an individual, if ever it recognizes the awesome success of God's forming them from dust, if ever my heart approaches the understanding of the price God paid to redeem individuals, if ever I understand that redemption is not for *nice* or *sweet* but for the worst sort of sinner, if ever…, then I will view people through compassionate eyes and will clothe myself with love and forgiveness.

Often we confuse civil rights with civil values. Good arguments are made for the rights of the individual in a free country. Unfortunately, these rights over which we argue mostly concern freedom to participate in debauchery. Though that may be called freedom, it certainly devalues the individual and places them in an "I don't care" category. Apathetic isolation opposes true value.

Jesus operated as a fully spirit-filled human being. John the Baptist informs us that the Spirit was given to him *without measure*. If we pay close attention, we will know what being filled with the Spirit might produce in our lives. I don't want to settle for anything less.

Chapter 26

Mary

Many scholars believe that Mary was only about 15 years old at the time she was betrothed to Joseph and at the time she received an angelic visitor with disturbing news—she was to have a son and she was not yet married. This virgin birth required a miracle, but, for God, this represented no difficulty.

How could Mary fit into our pattern of incompetents? How could she be described as among the *weak and foolish*? Mary's own song reveals an attitude where many have neglected to focus attention. She broke into this incredible song when she approached Elizabeth, her cousin, who was pregnant with John who would be called *The Baptist*.

And Mary said: "My soul glorifies the Lord
and my spirit rejoices in God my Savior,
for he has been mindful
of the humble state of his servant.
From now on all generations will call me blessed,
   for the Mighty One has done great things for
   me–
holy is his name.
His mercy extends to those who fear him,

from generation to generation.

He has performed mighty deeds with his arm; he
    has scattered those who are proud in their in-
    most thoughts.

He has brought down rulers from their thrones

but has lifted up the humble.

He has filled the hungry with good things

but has sent the rich away empty.

He has helped his servant Israel,

remembering to be merciful

to Abraham and his descendants forever,

even as he said to our fathers."

Luke 1:46–55

Mary recognized the state of her own humility and recognized that future declarations of blessed merely resulted from the Mighty One who had done great things for her. She sees the contrast between the privileged and the poor. She sees that the proud look forward only to being scattered, the rulers only to being brought down. The hungry feast on God's good things, the rich find their sack empty. Mercy is celebrated simply because she realizes that she and her people need mercy, a sign of weakness.

Mary's understanding of God and how he operates rings true—he comes to the humble and lowly. Surely, with this understanding, Mary would occupy a position of authority and oversight in the life of Jesus and in the early church. Surely the New Testament would be filled with quotes from her and with writers, leaders of the church indicating that they had verified theologies and actions with Mary. Not so!

Being the Mother of God at age 15 or 16 can be a heady thing perhaps even pushing her into being the typical *pushy mother*. Jesus certainly rebuked her on two recorded moments: First when she pushed him into performing a miracle to save a wedding party at Cana. Jesus has to say, *"Woman, what does your concern have to do with Me? My hour has not yet come."* (John 2:4 NKJ) Without missing a beat, Mary instructs the servants, *"Do whatever he tells you."* That is as pushy as you can get! However, Jesus, mercifully, saves the party.

Just Like a Mother

Further, when the family attended one of the main feasts in Jerusalem and returned toward Nazareth, after three days of journey, they discovered that the 12-year-old Jesus was not among the travelers. Frantically they return, finding him in the Temple in discussion with the rabbis, and, in typical motherly fashion, Mary says, *"Son, why have you treated us like this? Your father and I have been anxiously searching for you."* So, here Mary chastises God. Hmm. Jesus identifies her attitude for what it is by responding: *"Why were you searching for me? Didn't you know I had to be in my Father's house?"* (Luke 2:48-49)

You would think that with the messages from God and miracles of birth and protection in the past would have set their hearts in a direction of understanding. Again, not so! Here is the Bible's commentary on their anxiety: *"But they did not understand what he was saying to them."*

Though Mary pondered this event, along with others, in her heart she lacked understanding on another great moment. In Mark 3, the crowds so pressed Jesus that he was unable to eat lunch. This caused the family to decide that Jesus had lost his mind and they came to get him, take him home and get him well. (I guess that Jesus was so much into eating that not doing so totally shocked the family. I like that. Remember that they did call him a glutton, so he must have had a reputation for eating.)

When Mary and the brothers of Jesus arrive to get their sick boy and take him home, Jesus, from the middle of the crowd had great opportunity to affirm their concern and elevate Mary. Again, not so! Here is the description:

> Then Jesus' mother and brothers arrived. Standing outside, they sent someone in to call him. A crowd was sitting around him, and they told him, "Your mother and brothers are outside looking for you."

> "Who are my mother and my brothers?" he asked.

Then he looked at those seated in a circle
around him and said, "Here are my mother
and my brothers! Whoever does God's will
is my brother and sister and mother."
Mark 3:31–35

Jesus passes over the opportunity to elevate Mary to
any of the positions of go-between or co-redemptrix often espoused today. Instead, he relegates her and his
brothers to merely natural family while elevating those
who do God's will to his present and eternal family.
However we must pause and observe the gall of his family thinking that they could diagnose Jesus as crazy and
go get the Messiah to take home and rehabilitate.

Jesus bypasses another opportunity to elevate Mary
in the midst of his ministry on the earth:

As Jesus was saying these things, a woman
in the crowd called out, "Blessed is the
mother who gave you birth and nursed you."

He replied, "Blessed rather are those who
hear the word of God and obey it."
Luke 11:27–28

As Mary stands before the dying Jesus and observes
her hopes fading, Jesus places her under John's care as if
she were John's mother. Why John? Perhaps because
John also had a pushy mother and would be better
equipped to handle Mary. Perhaps.

Blessed Like the Rest

Finally, we see Mary for the last time among the 120 on the Day of Pentecost in that upper room waiting for the promise of the Father. Mary, as much as anyone else, needed the Holy Spirit to fill her life. No special endowment was given to her.

So the writers of the New Testament seemed to carefully ignore her. In no way was she ever elevated by the church. She found favor with God and was blessed. The blessings of God are not reserved for the mighty or sinless but are simply the outflow of our compassionate Creator. The world abounds with women who found favor with God and were blessed. I count my wife among that blessed group.

The last words of Mary, the ordinary, yet blessed, now 48-year-old, should still ring in our ears: *"Do whatever he tells you."*

Chapter 27

Job

Job presents a problem in our look at the incompetent and foolish. In spite of his friends who arrived equipped with condemnations over Job's terrible state, no sin appears to be laid to his charge. We only conjecture that in the end, his feeling that he could defend himself if he had an audience with God might ring of arrogance. This is borne out by God's simply reminding Job that some understanding exceeded the highest of his thinking. Obviously, God had to *yank his chain* in the end.

However, Job occupies the position of being the only person in the Bible, other than Jesus, of whom God actually boasts. In that strange narrative of the conversation with Satan, God's boasting of Job unleashes a torrent of suffering that, had Job been there, he might have voted against. I confess a lack of understanding over this conversation, although I think the theme of Job is the question, "Why do the righteous suffer?" and God chooses not to give us much of an answer. So, I leave it at that and pray that, whatever happens, Satan will underestimate me.

This question of boasting refuses to leave my mind. What about Job might cause God to boast? The fact that Job was fabulously wealthy holds me back a bit. If for no other reason, it seems that Job doesn't fit the *weak and foolish* thinking, even though it seems obvious that God had been the source of Job's prosperity.

I believe Job opens the door of understanding as he speaks of vindicating himself before God if only he could get a hearing. Listen to how Job describes his behavior:

> "How I long for the months gone by, for the days when God watched over me, when his lamp shone upon my head and by his light I walked through darkness! Oh, for the days when I was in my prime, when God's intimate friendship blessed my house, when the Almighty was still with me and my children were around me, when my path was drenched with cream and the rock poured out for me streams of olive oil.

> "When I went to the gate of the city and took my seat in the public square, the young men saw me and stepped aside and the old men rose to their feet; the chief men refrained from speaking and covered their mouths with their hands; the voices of the nobles were hushed, and their tongues stuck to the roof of their mouths. Whoever heard me spoke well of me, and those who saw me commended me, because I rescued the poor who cried for help, and the fatherless who had none to assist him. The man who was dying blessed me; I made the widow's heart sing. I put on righteousness as my clothing;

justice was my robe and my turban. I was eyes to the blind and feet to the lame. I was a father to the needy; I took up the case of the stranger. I broke the fangs of the wicked and snatched the victims from their teeth.

"I thought, 'I will die in my own house, my days as numerous as the grains of sand. My roots will reach to the water, and the dew will lie all night on my branches. My glory will remain fresh in me, the bow ever new in my hand.'

"Men listened to me expectantly, waiting in silence for my counsel. After I had spoken, they spoke no more; my words fell gently on their ears. They waited for me as for showers and drank in my words as the spring rain. When I smiled at them, they scarcely believed it; the light of my face was precious to them. I chose the way for them and sat as their chief; I dwelt as a king among his troops; I was like one who comforts mourners.

Job 29:2-25

First, Job reminisces about the *presence and fellowship of God* he enjoyed in times past and how blessing and prosperity followed his walk. He knew the reality of God and what he suffered now seemed unreal.

Second, Job reveals that he was so *wise* as a leader and politician (oh, to see that again) that when he arrived at the halls of congress, he was an automatic majority. All others withheld their comments and their vote. If Job voted for it, then it was right and must be done. How different from politicians who merely claim a walk with God but still run on God's platform ultimately embarrassing the kingdom of God. However, Job's reputation was unimpeachable.

Third, Job begins his actual defense by revealing why his reputation was so high. Job *rescued the poor and the orphans*. Now, rescued means much more that simply making a donation at the office. When he rescued them, that meant they had no further worries. Under Job's care no questions arose as from where the next meal might come. Being rescued meant they no longer lived in danger or in want.

Here Job reveals the direction of his heart and the direction that power flowed from him. He did not gather the poor and orphans into an army to empower himself or for him to exploit. Obviously, Job cared about people.

Fourth, the persons in the throes of death found their *hospice in Job*. They blessed Job probably because during their lives they had been beneficiaries of Job's generosity. How incredible that Job made the dying of men a time for blessings to flow. Perhaps, if there were such a place as a hospital, it might have been in the house of Job.

Fifth, he *made the widow's heart sing*. In ancient times, a widow simply starved to death unless she had a son or relative who cared for her. No social programs existed for her survival. Except for Job. Like the poor and fatherless, when Job found a helpless widow, she had no other worries. But she had plenty of time to rejoice and sing.

Sixth, *righteousness and justice* walked with him as clothing and uniforms. Job could not be bribed. No lobbyist came near him. No favoritism clouded his judgment. In his court everyone received justice. No arbitrary law or custom limited his thinking or put him in bondage. He knew what was right and acted accordingly.

Seventh, he was *eyes to the blind.* Schools did not exist for the blind nor did training programs assist them in self support. To their family, the blind were a burden, but not to Job. Perhaps Job gladly used his God-given wealth to hire someone who would provide the eyes to the blind, to care for them and educate them, to maintain their lives and give them hope and friendship.

Eighth, he was *feet to the lame.* No surgeons existed then to repair bones bent by birth or broken by labor. The future for the lame was a street corner and a cup. Their only hope was for a coin or two. That is, until Job arrived. Suddenly, their hope flourished. Their opportunities abounded…as if they had feet. How many people did Job hire just to be the sidekick for a lame person and make sure their life was as easy as possible and their transportation as sure as any walker? How many people did Job check on to see how they were doing? How deeply involved did he become with each person of need? We don't know, but you can see why the dying might bless him.

Ninth, he was *father to the needy*. Needy covers a lot of territory. Perhaps because he used the term *father*, Job is letting us know that those whose families presented damaging influence or whose personalities limited their capabilities or whose emotions kept them in chains found a caring overseer in him. Perhaps he spent time re-parenting those with faulty parents. Perhaps Job became the source of opportunity for the creative mind. Whatever the need, the answer was Job.

Tenth, he *took up the case of the stranger*. Being a stranger in an ancient land was a precarious and dangerous situation. A stranger could be mistreated or enslaved or ejected or even killed and no court bothered for justice because he was *just a stranger*. Few positions were more powerless than being a stranger. Except for Job. Job became the defense attorney for the stranger and, since we know he was a man of justice and his counsel was followed, the stranger suddenly had the rights of a family member. No one but Job had such a heart.

Eleventh, he *broke the fangs of the wicked and snatched the victims from their teeth*. Simply put, Job was the policeman of his area of influence. When he saw something evil happening to another, Job didn't wait for a committee meeting to discuss more personnel or to isolate the evildoer. Job actively interfered to oppose the wicked and save the innocent and powerless. Many victims are in the grip of wicked people today but the hands of the police are tied because they "haven't observed them breaking a law." Job, in his wisdom, knew and rescued.

Twelfth, Job's political influence was not the result of his being a "mover and shaker" nor was it his ability to hammer people into submission or manipulate them by fear. His wisdom and love made him everyone's favorite. *In his presence you knew you were safe.*

Thirteenth, Job *comforted mourners.* Mourners are those who have suffered loss and feel great distress. If one suffered loss financially, Job was there as a help to the needy. If one suffered loss of a loved one, Job was there as a father. In his presence, there was no loss.

As I look at this list, I begin to understand why God was proud of him. Job's wealth matched the commands of God. He never hoarded nor withheld yet never lacked. Stingy never described him. He never viewed his wealth as his own.

Job built no walls around his prosperity. He knew he owed his prosperity to God and seemed to understand how God cared for people. He was better than any government could be. If only the halls of our own government were made up of men like Job. That will not happen until the government rests upon the shoulders of Jesus.

Again, simply put, wherever Job had influence no needs existed, no one lacked, no one worried. His heart was turned, as is God's, toward the incompetent, the unfortunate, the weak, the lowly, the foolish. This others-centered life matched the nature of Jesus more than any person I see in the Bible except for Jesus himself.

Perhaps in his righteousness and suffering and loss of all things and then God raising him up, Job presents more of a type of Christ than any other character in the Bible. At least we know that God was proud.

Chapter 28

Shepherds and Kings

Let me pose two questions as a foundation for this chapter. Why do shepherds hear the good news first and what actions do they take? Why do kings hear the good news last and what actions do they take?

> And there were shepherds living out in the fields nearby, keeping watch over their flocks at night. An angel of the Lord appeared to them, and the glory of the Lord shone around them, and they were terrified. But the angel said to them, "Do not be afraid. I bring you good news of great joy that will be for all the people. Today in the town of David a Savior has been born to you; he is Christ the Lord. This will be a sign to you: You will find a baby wrapped in cloths and lying in a manger."

> Suddenly a great company of the heavenly host appeared with the angel, praising God and saying, "Glory to God in the highest, and on earth peace to men on whom his favor rests."

> When the angels had left them and gone into heaven, the shepherds said to one

another, "Let's go to Bethlehem and see this thing that has happened, which the Lord has told us about."

So they hurried off and found Mary and Joseph, and the baby, who was lying in the manger. When they had seen him, they spread the word concerning what had been told them about this child, and all who heard it were amazed at what the shepherds said to them. But Mary treasured up all these things and pondered them in her heart. The shepherds returned, glorifying and praising God for all the things they had heard and seen, which were just as they had been told.
Luke 2:8-20

Because of this presence in Scripture and because of Jesus calling himself the *Good Shepherd*, we view shepherds in a much higher status than they were in reality in the days of Jesus. Shepherds, though appreciative, would probably find our view a bit humorous.

The fact is, as we briefly outline in the chapter entitled "David," shepherds were considered the lowest of the low in Bible times. No one trusted shepherds. When they walked through town things tended to disappear. No one trusted their word. When Jesus spoke of the *hireling* shepherd who readily abandoned the sheep, everyone understood what he meant. For Jesus to call himself the *Good Shepherd*, to most ears it sounded like mutually exclusive terms.

So, why did the announcement reach shepherds first? Since God reaches for the weak and foolish and lowly, it follows simple reason that the first search would seek out the lowest, the shepherd. Indeed, for God to exhibit his grace and mercy, he had to go to shepherds first. Had the announcement come to anyone higher on the social scale, shepherds could justifiably think that the good news was not available to them. God had to go to them first to show how wide his arms of compassion and salvation spread.

What did the shepherds do about this remarkable announcement? They questioned, believed, worshiped and spread the word. As a side thought, rarely (do you know of one?) do preachers of the Word come from Wall Street. Abundantly, you hear of people rescued from the dregs of life who gladly take up their Bibles and walking shoes and spread the Word.

Why would the message come to kings? Let us look at the best known example:

> After Jesus was born in Bethlehem in Judea, during the time of King Herod, Magi from the east came to Jerusalem and asked, "Where is the one who has been born king of the Jews? We saw his star in the east and have come to worship him."
>
> When King Herod heard this he was disturbed, and all Jerusalem with him. When he had called together all the people's chief priests and teachers of the law, he

asked them where the Christ was to be born. "In Bethlehem in Judea," they replied, "for this is what the prophet has written:

"'But you, Bethlehem, in the land of Judah, are by no means least among the rulers of Judah; for out of you will come a ruler who will be the shepherd of my people Israel.'"

Then Herod called the Magi secretly and found out from them the exact time the star had appeared. He sent them to Bethlehem and said, "Go and make a careful search for the child. As soon as you find him, report to me, so that I too may go and worship him."

After they had heard the king, they went on their way, and the star they had seen in the east went ahead of them until it stopped over the place where the child was. When they saw the star, they were overjoyed. On coming to the house, they saw the child with his mother Mary, and they bowed down and worshiped him. Then they opened their treasures and presented him with gifts of gold and of incense and of myrrh. And having been warned in a dream not to go back to Herod, they returned to their country by another route.

When they had gone, an angel of the Lord appeared to Joseph in a dream. "Get up," he said, "take the child and his mother and escape to Egypt. Stay there until I tell you, for Herod is going to search for the child to kill him."

So he got up, took the child and his mother during the night and left for Egypt, where he stayed until the death of Herod. And so was fulfilled what the Lord had said through the prophet: "Out of Egypt I called my son."

When Herod realized that he had been outwitted by the Magi, he was furious, and he gave orders to kill all the boys in Bethlehem and its vicinity who were two years old and under, in accordance with the time he had learned from the Magi. Then what was said through the prophet Jeremiah was fulfilled:

"A voice is heard in Ramah, weeping and great mourning, Rachel weeping for her children and refusing to be comforted, because they are no more."

Matthew 2:1–18

God withholds the good news from no one. Eligibility for the message belongs to every creature. Even kings and noblemen hear if they will let God within earshot. For King Herod to hear, the message piped through men of position and wisdom, the elite of another country. Kings entertain such people. Their message was wrapped in a question, "Where is he that is born king of the Jews?" That is not a question a reigning king wants to hear. Power is never given up willingly.

During a time of persecution and hostility I was suffering from some religious elitists, a famous reporter who covered the whole story approached me and asked what the problem was. He had read my writings and found them far too gentle to have elicited such a response. After a few minutes of conversation he remarked, "Now I understand. They feel that their power is threatened. You can touch a man's body or his money and get away with it, but touch his power and he will fight to the last."

The news of a succeeding king set Herod on edge. In his best show of diplomacy, he gathered the information the wise men wanted (how nice) and set them off with the request to inform him of the location so he, too, could come and worship. The spin for public consumption was so good. He could advertise how he had been hospitable to the wise men, had favored them by providing all the information they needed, and wanted to join in the worship. He cooperated fully with these investigators. Everything they wanted, he gave them. (My, how these words ring in my ears from today's politicians).

God's Mercy

What Herod failed to make public was his seething fury. When the wise men, much more in touch with God, heard God say not to go back to Herod, his fury broke out in massacre of children. So the shepherds, by God's mercy, heard, worshiped and spread the word. In spite of God's mercy, Herod heard, lied and killed.

Perhaps that is the difference between the shepherd and the king, the lowest and the highest, the poor and the politician. Even now, every time the Supreme Court of the United States has the church before the court, the church loses. With every decision wickedness wins. When Congress decides, the poor get poorer and the rich get richer. The powerless lose what power they have and the powerful gorge on more power.

The only court of justice the lowly have is God's court. I shall never forget a prophecy from a dear preacher in Illinois. To a handful of other pastors and with a look of intensity in his eyes that bordered on wildness, he said Richard Nixon had lied to the Blacks and the poor and had abandoned them. Then he said, "Nixon will not complete his term. He will resign. Because God is our only court of justice and we are praying." I had chill bumps when the resignation occurred and I still do when I think of those fateful days. *God is our only court of justice and we are praying.*

Chapter 29

Equality

The joke goes, "All men are created equal, but some are more equal than others."

The truth is that *"God is no respecter of persons."* (Acts 10:34 KJV) God has no favorites. He so loved the (whole) world that whosoever (anyone) believes (a choice) in him should not perish but have everlasting life. Since God is no respecter of persons, then he regards the lowliest of persons just as highly as you or a king.

Perhaps that is why Jesus said, *"As you have done it to the least of these... you have done it to me."* (Matthew 25:40) This is to reinforce in our understanding just how God views people, all people, any people. Apparently God so hates the apparatus of separation and ranking that this equalization becomes the focus of the preaching of John the Baptist. Here is the scripture:

> In the fifteenth year of the reign of Tiberius Caesar–when Pontius Pilate was governor of Judea, Herod tetrarch of Galilee, his brother Philip tetrarch of Iturea and Traconitis, and Lysanias tetrarch of Abilene–during the high priesthood of Annas and Caiaphas, the word of God came to John

son of Zechariah in the desert. He went into all the country around the Jordan, preaching a baptism of repentance for the forgiveness of sins. As is written in the book of the words of Isaiah the prophet:

"A voice of one calling in the desert,
'Prepare the way for the Lord,
make straight paths for him.
Every valley shall be filled in,
every mountain and hill made low.
The crooked roads shall become straight,
the rough ways smooth.
And all mankind will see God's salvation.'"
Luke 3:1-6

And the glory of the LORD will be revealed,
and all mankind together will see it.
For the mouth of the LORD has spoken.
Isaiah 40:4-5

Can you see the implications: *Every* valley *lifted*. *Every* mountain *reduced*. The crooked *straight*. The rough *leveled*. The rugged *smoothed*. *And* the glory of the Lord will be revealed. Perhaps the equalization and the glory go together. Jesus recognized no higher levels of humanity. Even the Pharisees observed that about Jesus. Listen to the Apostle Paul's view:

> The eye cannot say to the hand, "I don't need you!" And the head cannot say to the feet, "I don't need you!" On the contrary, those parts of the body that seem to be

weaker are indispensable, and the parts that we think are less honorable we treat with special honor. And the parts that are unpresentable are treated with special modesty, while our presentable parts need no special treatment. But God has combined the members of the body and has given greater honor to the parts that lacked it, so that there should be no division in the body, but that its parts should have equal concern for each other. If one part suffers, every part suffers with it; if one part is honored, every part rejoices with it.

1 Corinthians 12:21–26

Massive Egos

We give "greater honor to the parts (of the body) that lacked it"? No we don't! At least that is what I thought as I conversed with a wise pastor at a conference. I told him that this passage always bothered me.

"We have unpresentable parts of the body at our church but we do not give them greater honor. I think of them as visitors," I jokingly concluded.

"Then you are looking at this backward," my pastor friend stated. "You need to discover who gets the most honor at your church and then you will know who the most unpresentable are." That bowled me over.

"Well, I get the most honor and the elders would be next in honor," I mused.

"Precisely," he answered as a big grin enveloped his face.

Then I understood. When I am in a leadership position and when I am with such leaders, we are a collection of massive egos. We position and manipulate. We struggle to prove ourselves superior thinkers. We seek honor. This very ego-centeredness is the opposite of the nature of Jesus and the opposite of the way the Bible tells us to view ourselves.

The Uglies

This concept simply makes us the spiritual uglies. God knows this and permits or even bestows on us the honor to cover our ugliness. God has a way of leveling the mountain. I had it all wrong.

Some years ago, I received a brochure touting the development of a new network of young and up-and-coming leaders in the church. I was a bit cynical because I had not received an invitation to join but was merely asked who I would recommend. Harumph! But I was further put off by the very fact that a new elitism was being developed. Would their meetings be built around deciding who was the most up and coming? How would they decide if someone was more down and leaving? Would they ever do a servant network? Would a servant want to participate? Wouldn't such a network take time away from his servanthood?

I constantly receive (under cheap postage) notices that I have been chosen to be included in the "Who's Who" of whatever. All I have to do is fill out the form listing my memberships and accomplishments and include a photo of myself along with a significant amount of money to cover the cost of the book that will include my listing. What a brilliant way to grab the ego of a person and make money selling books to them. Now, if they ever invite me to be included in "Why Wasn't He a Who?" I might be interested.

I live in the valley of California that includes Palm Springs, its most famous city. The papers are filled with reports on the activities of the rich and famous. TV stations and newspapers hire individuals whose only job is to scope out the celebrities and tell what they are doing or where they are being seen.

I live in one of two cities of the desert where the poor people live who work for the rich people. They are the two largest cities in the valley. An upscale city next to mine engineered a trade of land so a much valued mountainside on which multimillion dollar houses would be built could be in the upscale city rather than mine.

No one would pay such a price if the address listed my city. I drive through a barrio to reach my house, yet from my house I can see the mountainside mansions. The *people* live in my town. And God loves people.

I watch as they build and keep thinking, "Every valley lifted, every mountain made low. If only they knew."

Chapter 30

The Poor You Have

While Jesus was in Bethany in the home of a man known as Simon the Leper, a woman came to him with an alabaster jar of very expensive perfume, which she poured on his head as he was reclining at the table.

When the disciples saw this, they were indignant. "Why this waste?" they asked. "This perfume could have been sold at a high price and the money given to the poor."

Aware of this, Jesus said to them, "Why are you bothering this woman? She has done a beautiful thing to me. The poor you will always have with you, but you will not always have me. When she poured this perfume on my body, she did it to prepare me for burial. I tell you the truth, wherever this gospel is preached throughout the world, what she has done will also be told, in memory of her."

Matthew 26:6–13

W hat a great excuse resides within this passage. How often I hear *The poor you will always have with you* given as a reason for not helping the poor right now. This was not a release given to the disciples but a rebuke. Were they truly interested in the poor, their prior actions would have been evidence. They were more interested in the income. Or more interested in criticizing. Or embarrassed to be in the presence of a questionable woman.

Occasionally I hear TV evangelists, in attempts to raise money, asking people to make an "alabaster box" sacrifice. I have never heard such a request made in order to help the poor—only the TV evangelist. Sometimes I hear people choosing to contribute to some great building or venture and using the excuse that the poor we have always, but we are doing this just for Jesus. Perhaps, but why do they want their name on the building or the plaque honoring them for the donation? What am I supposed to think when I hear a politician say we need to help the rich so they can hire the poor?

It is true that the poor will always be with us, but that simply means we will always have opportunity to exhibit the nature of Jesus in our generosity. The point further is that you will never lack a means of showing grace and mercy. We all have, in some way, an alabaster box. What shall the disposition be?

I once received a phone call from a person who voiced a complaint against a church where I had recently taught. He felt that the church did not do anything to help the poor. He was soliciting my agreement and hoping I would lobby the pastor to begin some sort of benevolence program. I simply asked one question, "Are you personally doing anything to help the poor?" He hesitantly answered, "No." Then I said, "You have no right to call me and say these things since you are not doing what you demand of others." The conversation was over. You will always have opportunity to identify with the lowly.

Chapter 31

The Remarkable Thread

Just as the scarlet thread of redemption winds through the Scripture, so winds the golden thread of humility. God's great writers recognized God's nature and carefully obeyed as they recorded the Word. Look at the thread as it develops into a rope:

> Seek the LORD, all you humble of the land,
> you who do what he commands.
> Seek righteousness, seek humility;...
> Zephaniah 2:3

None seemed to capture the thought better than Isaiah:

> The eyes of the arrogant man will be
> humbled
> and the pride of men brought low;
> the LORD alone will be exalted in that day.
> The LORD Almighty has a day in store
> for all the proud and lofty,
> for all that is exalted
> (and they will be humbled),...
> Isaiah 2:11–12

As we sing Handel's Messiah, these words march through our hearts. Nothing speaks the reality of God's view of things more than the statement that *every* hill shall be made low. Arrogance and elitism are doomed in the kingdom of God.

> Every valley shall be raised up,
>
> every mountain and hill made low;
>
> the rough ground shall become level,
>
> the rugged places a plain.
>
> And the glory of the LORD will be revealed,
>
> and all mankind together will see it.
>
> For the mouth of the LORD has spoken.
>
> Isaiah 40:4–5

To prove this humility by contrast, God records through Isaiah this awesome view of the heart of Satan, the pride and arrogance that formed the gap between Heaven and Hell:

> How you have fallen from heaven,
>
> O Lucifer, O morning star, son of the dawn!
>
> You have been cast down to the earth,
>
> you who once laid low the nations!
>
> You said in your heart,
>
> "I will ascend to heaven;
>
> I will raise my throne
>
> above the stars of God;
>
> I will sit enthroned on the mount of assembly,
>
> on the utmost heights of the sacred mountain.
>
> "I will ascend above the tops of the clouds;

I will make myself like the Most High."
But you are brought down to the grave,
to the depths of the pit.
Those who see you stare at you,
they ponder your fate:
"Is this the man who shook the earth
and made kingdoms tremble,
the man who made the world a desert,
who overthrew its cities
and would not let his captives go home?"
Isaiah 14:12–17

A brief look at some verses that provide strands of the rope of humility:

The LORD sends poverty and wealth;
he humbles and he exalts.
He raises the poor from the dust
and lifts the needy from the ash heap;
he seats them with princes
and has them inherit a throne of honor.
1 Samuel 2:7

> When they arrived, Samuel saw Eliab and thought,
> "Surely the LORD's anointed stands here before the LORD."
> But the LORD said to Samuel,

"Do not consider his appearance or his
height,
for I have rejected him.
The LORD does not look at the things man
looks at.
Man looks at the outward appearance, but
the LORD looks at the heart."
1 Samuel 16:6–7

To fear the LORD is to hate evil;
I hate pride and arrogance,
evil behavior and
perverse speech.
Proverbs 8:13

There are six things the LORD hates,
seven that are detestable to him:
haughty eyes,
a lying tongue,
hands that shed innocent blood,
a heart that devises wicked schemes,
feet that are quick to rush into evil,
a false witness who pours out lies
and a man who stirs up dissension among
brothers.
Proverbs 6:16–19

Before destruction
the heart of man is haughty, and
before honour is humility.
Proverbs 18:12 KJV

He has showed you, O man, what is good.
And what does the LORD require of you?
To act justly and to
love mercy and to
walk humbly with your God.
Micah 6:8

Do nothing
out of selfish ambition
or vain conceit, but
in humility
consider others
better than yourselves.
Philippians 2:3

But he gives us more grace.
That is why Scripture says:
"God opposes the proud but
gives grace to the humble."
James 4:6

Humble yourselves before the Lord, and
he will lift you up.
James 4:10

If anyone thinks he is something
when he is nothing,
he deceives himself.
Galatians 6:3

Your beauty should not come
from outward adornment,
such as braided hair and
the wearing of gold jewelry
and fine clothes.
Instead,
it should be that of your inner self,
the unfading beauty
of a gentle and quiet spirit,
which is of great worth in God's sight.
1 Peter 3:3–4

We continue to march through a gallery of God's losers, the weak, the foolish, the humble, the kind of people he can use, and observe our heroes with new insight.

Chapter 32

The Exact Likeness

*The Son is the radiance of God's glory and the exact representation of his being. (*Hebrews 1:3)

Many people view God as issuing orders from heaven then punishing by massive disasters those who didn't hear or disobeyed. Ah, but the God we know, the one who is true and faithful made himself available through his son who was exactly like him. So, in order to see God accurately, we watch his son.

I believe the most concise expression of the *Nature of Jesus* comes from his *greatest in the kingdom* teachings which I relate in greater detail in **The Jesus Style**, a book I consider to be my most important and which has received the greatest distribution. However, the verses that condense his nature to the most concise form are Matthew 20:25-28:

> "You know that the rulers of the Gentiles lord it over them, and those who are great exercise authority over them. Yet it shall not be so among you; but whoever desires to become great among you, let him be your servant. And whoever desires to be first among you, let him be your slave—just as the Son of

Man did not come to be served, but to serve, and to give His life a ransom for many." NKJ

The greatest in the universe becomes the least and serves us. Jesus was truly the one servant-hearted, others-centered person. In this manner, he revealed the exact nature of God, the Father. Here is the compilation of Jesus' own teachings about his greatness:

1. Servant or Slave.
   Matthew 20:25-28; Matthew 23:11;
   Mark 9:33-35, 10:43-45
2. Did Not *Lord It Over* Others.
   Matthew 20:20-28; Luke 22:24
3. Led by Example.
   Matthew 20:28, 23:1-4; John 13:12-17
4. Humble.
   Matthew 18:1-5, 23:12; Luke 14:11
5. As a Child.
   Matthew 18:1-5; Luke 9:46-48
6. As the Younger.
   Luke 22:24-27
7. As the Least.
   Luke 9:46-48
8. As the Last.
   Matthew 20:16; Mark 9:33-35

As Jesus unfolded his ministry, his teaching and life remained consistent. Such consistency kept Jesus and the ruling religious leaders at constant odds:

"Woe to you Pharisees, because you love the most important seats in the synagogues and greetings in the marketplaces."
Luke 11:43

The Pharisees, who loved money, heard all this and were sneering at Jesus. He said to them, "You are the ones who justify yourselves in the eyes of men, but God knows your hearts. What is highly valued among men is detestable in God's sight."
Luke 16:14–15

I am personally most troubled by Jesus' statement: *"What is highly valued among men is detestable in God's sight."* When this first struck home in my heart, I wanted to disappear for a long time and just ponder. Few things rearrange my life more than dealing with that statement. However, when you watch Jesus, he lived what he taught. Though he could have had anything/everything he wanted (keep in mind that since he was tempted in all points as we are, he *wanted* everything), he relinquished it all for our sakes so he could walk with us and truly be Emanuel—God with us.

As proof of his love for people and as part of his teaching about himself in the *greatest in the kingdom* teachings, he gives the apostles a shocking lesson:

At that time the disciples came to Jesus and asked, "Who is the greatest in the kingdom of heaven?"

He called a little child and had him stand among them. And he said: "I tell you the truth, unless you change and become like little children, you will never enter the kingdom of heaven. Therefore, whoever humbles himself like this child is the greatest in the kingdom of heaven.

"And whoever welcomes a little child like this in my name welcomes me. But if anyone causes one of these little ones who believe in me to sin, it would be better for him to have a large millstone hung around his neck and to be drowned in the depths of the sea." Matthew 18:1-6

At one point, the erroneous view the apostles held toward children and mothers exhibited their nature, which resulted in disciplinary teaching by Jesus. I wonder what *indignant* truly describes.

People were bringing little children to Jesus to have him touch them, but the disciples rebuked them. When Jesus saw this, he was indignant. He said to them, "Let the little children come to me, and do not hinder them, for the kingdom of God belongs to such as these. I tell you the truth, anyone who will not receive the kingdom of God

like a little child will never enter it." And he took the children in his arms, put his hands on them and blessed them.
Mark 10:13-16

Jesus constantly surrounded the needy with his presence, touching the untouchable, eating with sinners, healing the hopeless. Every phase of his walk in the flesh showed his love for people and his disdain for those who had oppressed them. What he offered could come only from a loving heart:

> "Come to me, all you who are weary and burdened, and I will give you rest. Take my yoke upon you and learn from me, for I am gentle and humble in heart, and you will find rest for your souls. For my yoke is easy and my burden is light." Matthew 11:28-30

As Jesus describes himself as gentle and humble, my heart leaps into his care. Where else can I go? Writers of the Scripture return repeatedly to the *Nature of Jesus* for reasons I understand. I cannot learn enough of him and I want to speak only of him. Paul also explodes with this wonderful passage:

> Let this mind be in you which was also in Christ Jesus, who, being in the form of God, did not consider it robbery to be equal with God, but made himself of no reputation, taking the form of a bondservant, and coming in the likeness of men. And being found in appearance as a man, he humbled himself

and became obedient to the point of death, even the death of the cross. Therefore God also has highly exalted him and given him the name which is above every name, that at the name of Jesus every knee should bow, of those in heaven, and of those on earth, and of those under the earth, and that every tongue should confess that Jesus Christ is Lord, to the glory of God the Father.
Philippians 2:5–11 NKJ

The previous passage permits us to add six more items to our *greatest in the kingdom* list:

9. Used No Force on Us.
10. Was Not Driven by Selfish Ambition.
11. Made Himself of No Reputation.
12. Fully Human.
13. Obedient.
14. Even Unto Death.

Actually, because Jesus paid the price of death for our sins, and rose from the dead, we freely add to our list of *greatest in the kingdom* understandings.

15. Raised to Life.

Jesus took unique and purposeful steps to make himself of no reputation, a necessary set of acts in order for us to be comfortable with him.

1. He was born in a barn.

2. He had what we would call questionable parents.

3. He had a very common name.

4. His announcement came to the lowest of humans.

5. He was not handsome.

6. He grew up in a bad neighborhood.

7. He owned nothing.

8. He had a strange advance-man.

9. His cabinet/crew was of little use.

10. He died a very bad and embarrassing death.

All of this he did just so he could reach as far as *me* and make me feel welcome in his presence. All this just so I could clearly see the Father. All this just so I, and anyone else who chooses to believe, could be redeemed and changed and raised up from my lowliness and death to be with him.

Chapter 33

First and Final

When you look at the ancestry of Jesus, you find it filled with the sort of people who deserve to be discreetly ignored. Instead, Scripture celebrates them. When you study the heroes of Scripture, you discover one despised or incompetent person after another.

When you trace the style of God, searching for his type of person, you find a consistent penchant for the outcast and the rejected. A simple reading of the passages in Isaiah 61 and Luke 4 reveals the people for whom the heart of the Lord beats—the poor, the brokenhearted, the captives, the prisoner, the blind, the out-of-favor, the mourner. For those who wish to harvest the cream of their demographics, now they know who they are.

Further, Jesus kindly issues a formal invitation to the upper echelon of people—those who can never claim lack of opportunity—only to receive ridiculous turndowns which certainly exposes the direction of their hearts. In response to this rejection from the social register, Jesus instructs, as the master of the feast, that his workers now seek out the alley dwellers, the poor, the crippled, the lame. (Luke 14:15-24)

The space allotted for this banquet still cries out for more guests, so the servants now leave the cities and walk the country roads and lanes to reach those who have little or no access to the latest news or who cannot afford city life.

Even further, in Matthew 11:28, Jesus invites the labored and heavily-laden one, the weary and the burdened down. In every town and village Jesus healed sick people and others who had no hope while, at the same time, Jesus was suffering the attacks of the wealthy and powerful.

Then Jesus reveals the heart from which all this compassion flows: *"...I am gentle and humble in heart, and you will find rest for your souls. For my yoke is easy and my burden is light."* (Matthew 11:29-30) Jesus, who walked among the disadvantaged, understood the plight of people and cared for them.

The Scripture gives adequate evidence of the status of Jesus. John, the beloved, tells us: *"The Word became flesh and dwelt among us."* (John 1:14 NKJ)

John had no physical or economic clues to tell him that Jesus was the Messiah—only the anointing of the Holy Spirit. (John 1:29-34)

Jesus was made *"in the likeness of sinful flesh."* (Romans 8:3 NKJ)

Paul says of Jesus, he *"made himself nothing, taking the very nature of a servant, being made in human likeness. And being found in appearance as a man, he humbled himself...."* (Philippians 2:7-8)

To put the final clues together, the writer of Hebrews reveals two major facets of the status of Jesus. *For this reason he had to be* **made like his brothers in every way,** *in order that he might become a merciful and faithful high priest in service to God and that he might make atonement for the sins of the people. Because he himself suffered when he was tempted, he is able to help those who are being tempted.* (Hebrews 2:17-18 emphasis mine)

So, since Jesus was just like us in every way and suffered the same temptations we do (in fact, every temptation), he understands us and we can understand the source of his compassion. Kings and congresses of this world seek the wealthy and influential and capable who can finance their wars and line their pockets.

The King of kings seeks the rest of us.

Chapter 34

Heaven Before Heaven

One scary problem faces me. I could never in my life reproduce what Jesus did. My spiritual resume is a string of failures and crashes. Perhaps you find it easy to identify with the common folk and hard to rise above your failures and inabilities and incompetences. Take courage and embrace hope. Since God made us, he knows that our building blocks are but dust, and the flesh profits nothing. To my joy, as if God knew my incapacity, he planted my instructions of hope in Scripture. I may not be mighty, but I can lean on the Mighty One!

...for it is God who works in you both to will and to do for His good pleasure. Philippians 2:13 NKJ

Ahhh!

...He who has begun a good work in you will complete it until the day of Jesus Christ; Philippians 1:6 NKJ

Ahhh!

...looking unto Jesus, the author and finisher of our faith. Hebrews 12:2 NKJ

Ahhh!

And we,..., are being transformed into his likeness with ever-increasing glory, which comes from the Lord, who is the Spirit. 2 Corinthians 3:18

Ahhh!

And God raised us up with Christ and seated us with him in the heavenly realms in Christ Jesus, in order that in the coming ages he might show the incomparable riches of his grace, expressed in his kindness to us in Christ Jesus. Ephesians 2:6-7

Ahhh!

For it is by grace you have been saved, through faith—and this not from yourselves, it is the gift of God-not by works, so that no one can boast. For we are God's workmanship, ... Ephesians 2:8-10

Ahhh!

If you remain in me and my words remain in you, ask whatever you wish, and it will be given you. John 15:7

Ahhh!

Therefore, since through God's mercy we have this ministry, we do not lose heart. 2 Corinthians 4:1

Ahhh!

A bit of Heaven to go to Heaven in. I no longer need worry about my incompetence. Life is *all* of him.

Additional Books and Resources
By Gayle D. Erwin

The Jesus Style
Now in more than 45 printings in English and 35 languages, this classic remains a favorite for Christian growth. Required in many schools and churches. A choice gift.

The Father Style
Fresh view of his Grace, Mercy, Name and Glory.

The Spirit Style
A healing and resolving look at the whole of the Spirit's work.

The Body Style
Looking at the Church through the eyes of the Founder.

Handbook for Servants
Priceless help for those who want to be like Jesus.

That Reminds Me of A Story
Forty unique true stories from Gayle's life and observation.

That Reminds Me of Another Story
Fifty more unique and true stories from Gayle's life and observation.

Audio and Video
Hours of dramatic, humorous and memorable scriptural teaching on video DVD and audio CD plus audio MP3. Appeals to all ages.

Available through:

Servant Quarters, PO Box 219, Cathedral City, CA 92235

Order toll free at 1-888-321-0077

Web site: www.servant.org

Email: gayle@servant.org